MW00456278

SACRA DOCTRINA

Christian Theology for a Postmodern Age

www.ctrf.info

SACRA DOCTRINA

Christian Theology for a Postmodern Age

BEING PROMISED

Theology, Gift, and Practice

Gregory Walter

WILLIAM B. EERDMANS PUBLISHING COMPANY
GRAND RAPIDS, MICHIGAN / CAMBRIDGE, U.K.

Wm. B. Eerdmans Publishing Co.
2140 Oak Industrial Drive N.E., Grand Rapids, Michigan 49505 /
P.O. Box 163, Cambridge CB3 9PU U.K.

Printed in the United States of America

19 18 17 16 15 14 13   7 6 5 4 3 2 1

Library of Congress Cataloging-in-Publication Data

Walter, Gregory, 1974-
Being promised: theology, gift, and practice / Gregory Walter.
pages   cm. — (Sacra doctrina:
Christian theology for a postmodern age)
Includes bibliographical references and index.
ISBN 978-0-8028-6415-4 (pbk.: alk. paper)
1. God (Christianity) — Promises. 2. Gifts —
Religious aspects — Christianity.   I. Title.

BT180.P7W35   2013

231.7 — dc23

2013018817

www.eerdmans.com

To Grete,
In the midst of the liturgy of the everyday,
there you are,
uncommon grace.

Contents

Foreword:
Attending to Being Promised

"Keep awake and pray that you may not come into the time of trial; the spirit indeed is willing, but the flesh is weak."

Mark 14:38

"I freely confess that it was the objection of David Hume that first, many years ago, interrupted my dogmatic slumber."

Immanuel Kant, *Prolegomena to Any Future Metaphysics*

"Life is a blur, focus on style."

Advertisement in *New York Times Magazine*

Keep awake. Pay attention. Know where you are and the time in which you live. Gregory Walter's book heeds this contemporary, although also perennial, call to attentiveness. If you are a reader who wishes to answer this call, who struggles to be wise and awake within the buzz and blur of our time of plurality, diversity, ambiguity, and ambivalence, this book is for you.

True attentiveness involves at least four layers of reflective focus. First, you will want to attend to the layer of everyday practices of life as they present themselves. An example from my days as a young pastor on the South Side of Chicago comes to mind: a young woman (14 years of age) sitting in your office and telling you, "I am pregnant." You might immediately attend to the seemingly ordinary habits of contemporary life often taken for granted, such as: How far is she along in the pregnancy? Is there a father who will be part of this conversation? How does the woman feel about the pregnancy? Does she see it as gift or curse? Have any promises been given or received by the young woman and the father of the child? Are they likely to be kept? So many feelings and thoughts crowd your attention in the buzz and blur of such moments. Nonetheless, you cannot escape thinking about these particular and ordinary questions. And you are impatient with abstract thoughts that escape these ordinary realities. This young woman's family system, and the forces of class, race, culture, and community, now center upon her as she confesses, "I am pregnant."

Second, at a deeper layer, you need to attend to emerging commonsense rules and patterns that make such day-to-day habits and practices more nimble and resilient than the initial and often overwhelming force of the immediacy of the reality that she is pregnant. These rules and patterns might, in her setting, be thought to be "common sense" in a contemporary culture where nothing is quite as uncommon as common sense. Rather than succumbing to unreflective practices and habits, as someone who is paying careful attention (or, carefully attending to this environment) you see such rules and patterns at play. For example: Do not kill. Do no harm. Do what is best for you. They will begin to shape this young woman's likely options: she can abort this child; she can choose the child's adoptive parents in an open adoption; she can keep the child and raise it with the father or with her extended family or on her own; or, in her despair about her circumstances, she can commit suicide. Other options might well exist, but these are the ones you ponder as you attend to her and her dilemma.

Third, you will want to attend to the theories that make sense of these commonsense rules and patterns. These theories seek communion with the practical circumstances of this young woman and the rules that you have considered without forsaking your desire for theoretical coherence and truth seeking. Your attentiveness risks a more critical relationship with the previous two layers. In being an ethical companion to the young woman, you will consider such difficult and tragic questions as these: What is life? What is worthy of being treated as human? Is life a gift from God? Does such a gift create obligations? If promises, either implied or explicit, have been made, does this change how these other questions are understood?

Fourth, you will need to attend to the deep structures that lie beneath the ordinary practices and habits. These deep structures even shape your theories, indeed, your theory making. Some call these deep structures "metatheoretical." Others describe them as the fundamental exigencies of our life world. One of these fundamental exigencies in this instance is suffering and death. For some, death is the only or the greatest enemy, to be avoided no matter what the cost in suffering. For others, suffering is the only or greatest enemy and even death is better than continuing to suffer. Another fundamental exigency is the experience of receiving a gift or being promised. At the root of any society lies the necessity of the giving and receiving of gifts and the giving, receiving, and keeping or failing to keep promises. Without these necessary actions, trust fails and eventually so does the viability of such a society. No matter how the next moments, days, and years unfold for this young woman as you work with her, these exigencies will be played out.

Gregory Walter's book focuses especially on one of these fundamental exigencies, the dynamic of promising and being promised. Making promises is a day-to-day practice and habit. Without promises, life does not move into the future. Those who refuse to make or to keep their promises frustrate the work God does with us to build a trustworthy world in everyday ways. The absence or failure of promise can easily break down the most basic human activities toward a healthy life for others and oneself.

Gregory Walter's book brings us into the interplay of promising and being the one to whom a promise is given by considering the rituals of gift exchange found in all human cultures. He draws upon a century of reflection by anthropologists on cultural practices of gift exchange and at least a half-century of reflection by philosophers centered on the search for the "pure gift" that does not oblige the receiver to make a return gift. He brings that reflection into conversation with emerging readings of the Christian Scriptures on the gift, particularly the giving of a gracious God and the experience of one who receives the promise from that God.

The attentive and patient reader of this book will embark on a journey that delights, moves, and teaches. Perhaps the most careful rendering of our human condition as persons who have received this promise, the book unfolds with gentle patience and grace. Like a fine jeweler, Walter polishes the diverse facets of the practices of promising and receiving a promise in much the same fashion that my teacher Paul Ricoeur pursued in his hermeneutical phenomenology. Rather than simply analyzing the phenomena of gift exchange and giving and receiving a promise, Walter unfolds its layers of reflection on this scholarship with nuance and care; his argument invites insights rather than coerces conclusions. The result is a journey through canonical works on gift and recipient seen through a distinct and unmistakable Christian vision into the necessity for trust in the unconditional promise of life in Jesus Christ that flows out of our reality that we are promised by God. For me, Walter's generous polishing and evocative questioning speak to the need to deepen my own trusting of this unconditional promise and to proclaim that promise to a world of people caught in the buzz and blur of contemporary life. In that, this book is nothing short of exhilarated insight and renewed hope for the church's unique part of God's mission in the world. It is profoundly promising.

Patrick R. Keifert
August 2013

Acknowledgments

This book tries to answer a question that emerged while I was an undergraduate taking my first theology class. Robert W. Jenson, the instructor of that class, probed this important question: What is this promise that is the gospel of Jesus? Similarly, the late Gerhard O. Forde provocatively opened up for me the connections between the question of promise and Martin Luther's own theology. These questions also received considerable shape from a Ph.D. dissertation at Princeton Theological Seminary that attended to the recovery of promise by Hans Joachim Iwand. I wrote that dissertation under the supervision of Bruce L. McCormack, who constantly urged me to consider the systematic and constructive issues that attend promise. The following friends gave time, comments, and suggestions for improving the project and manuscript: Marc Kolden, Gary Simpson, Clint Schnekloth, Peder Jothen, Jamie Schillinger, Douglas Casson, Christian Collins-Winn, David Hahn, and Matthew Martin Nickoloff. Patrick R. Keifert has graciously written a foreword to this work, which is hardly the only matter for which I owe him thanks.

Finally, I continuously benefit from the creative and remarkable ways in which the students I have taught at St. Olaf College have responded to these ideas as we have explored them in theological writings, novels, and film. Though I owe all these students, teachers, and fellow theologians many debts, and I surely have not counted them all, the errors that remain are my own.

I thank Jon Pott, Editor-in-Chief of Wm. B. Eerdmans Publishing, and Alan Padgett for accepting this book in the Sacra Doctrina series. I further thank the editors of Wm. B. Eerdmans for their work in improving the manuscript and seeing it through to publication. I am grateful to President David Anderson and the Regents of St. Olaf College for granting me a sabbatical in the year 2011-2012 which enabled me to complete the manuscript. At St. Olaf College, I participated in a faculty seminar, led by Margaret Odell, where I presented these ideas in early form and received much aid from my departmental colleagues. Gary Stansell, in particular, graciously held a seminar with me on gift.

I am grateful to the editors of the *Journal of Lutheran Ethics* for permission to use, in edited form, portions of my essay "Recognizing the Other in Liturgical Acts: Pluralism and Eucharist," *Journal of Lutheran Ethics* 10, no. 9 (2010). I am also grateful to Bloodaxe Books for permission to use part of Gillian Allnutt's poem "Sarah's Laughter." All translations are my own unless otherwise indicated. Biblical quotations are from the New Revised Standard Version.

While I was revising chapter 4, I read a remarkable paragraph that sums up better than I could the kind of practical orientation enabled by promise. I wish to quote it in full since it so carefully and beautifully gives the moral *sensorium* that promise shapes:

> Christians in their longing for Christ find themselves deeply immersed in the sufferings of the world. Christians are not aloof spectators, watching the world's troubles. Faith in Christ does not give special knowledge that trumps the reasoning power of those leading civil institutions. What faith does do is to lead us into solidarity with suffering. The groaning of creation is our groaning just as the Spirit of God sighs our sighs (Romans 8:18-39). That is why we, by the Spirit and out of faith, eagerly anticipate and await the justice of the gospel (Galatians 5:5). Until Christ's return, however, the Spirit of God does not let us say "has been done." (Evangelical Lutheran Church in America, *Draft Statement on Criminal Justice*, 2012, p. 19)

I would not have been able to complete this book without Grete Walter. Since the beginning of our friendship and continuing on into our marriage, she has been a counselor in perplexity and a giver of uncommon grace. With her, we now have a busy home of which this book is just a small piece. Our two sons, Carsten and Erik, make up the larger part of our home. I could hardly write on promise without being constantly delighted and surprised by the gifts and tasks given by these two. They each brim with promise and train Grete and me to expect the unexpected.

Gregory Walter
St. Olaf College
Northfield, Minnesota

On the Commemoration of Columba, Aiden, and Bede,
Teachers and Renewers of the Church
9 June 2013

CHAPTER 1

Promise, Speech-Acts, and Gifts

Multa fidem promissa leuant.

Horace, *Epistulae*

The poet Horace wrote several letters to reflect with his interlocutors about the tasks of writing drama and poetry. He offered several principles that would lead a writer to compose a play whose characters and action had the best chance of eliciting an appropriate response from their audience. Among these many reflections, he held that a playwright must not promise too much. "Lavish promises lessen credit," he wrote, meaning that pledging too much can lead a person to risk his or her credibility.[1] If the promises get too wild, too out of hand, they verge on madness and fancy. They would fuel fantasy and strip sense. Such a situation could fail utterly to convince anyone that the promising character or that the implicit promise of the plot would be worth belief.

Three strangers visited Sarah and Abraham, pledging a son. Their promise was too lavish and Sarah laughed. To this, the visitors responded, "Is anything too wonderful for YHWH?" This God who promises does so lavishly, transgressing Horace's firm limits for a good story and a fair practice. God's promise repeats with and beyond this ancient scripture, credible or not, wonderful beyond measure but hidden, masked, and mixed with the lowly and ordinary.

If impossible, this promise is God's. If incredible, promise engenders belief beyond belief, if there is a promise worthy of the name.

1. Horace, *Epistulae* 2.2.

1.1. Introduction

We rely on promises. This is true no matter if they are ordinary human ones or the kind that are repeated and called the good news about Jesus, as Mark describes the promise of God in his gospel. These acts bind us together and the pledge or oath that they make seems to hold even to the end of our life. Promise, along with gift, is among the predominant metaphors the Western Christian tradition uses to describe God's gracious actions.

Since promise is pervasive, it risks being commonplace. For promise to have its place in theology and practice, it requires attention and examination. To be sure, the practice and concept is evident throughout the Bible, whether in an explicit form, as in the promise to Sarah and Abraham, or in such complex matters such as covenant, law, and the massive use of promise throughout the gospels and the epistles. It has played many roles in the history of theology.[2] It has prominence in medieval reflection on the sacraments and it has had powerful repercussions on the way that Christians have related to and understood Jewish peoples. Most sharply of all, Martin Luther has given promise a decisive place, not merely for developing doctrines but also in the mission of the church: to repeat and communicate God's promise.[3]

In order to attend to promise again, to bring it to light, I shall show how promise is a gift. Many theologians have brought to the fore discourses of gift-exchange in recent decades in order to articulate God's actions or graciousness, as well as to show the practical implications of theological claims. Indeed, grace is semantically linked to gift throughout their mutual history, even when they have been radically distinguished. These attempts to make use of gift in theology are various and follow considerably divergent theological paths. What unites them is the recent prominence of practice in constructive systematic theology and attention to the latter's post-metaphysical tasks. The emergence of practice has come in many various ways and certainly gift-exchange is one of them. Numerous theologians have explored the ways to integrate gift-exchange into theology and the church's mission.[4]

---

2. On the history of promise in philosophy and theology, see Heinrich Assel, "Verheissung," in *Historisches Wörterbuch der Philosophie*, vol. 11 (Basel: Schwabe Verlag, 2001), pp. 689-94. For a history of promise in the late medieval and early Reformation theology, see Berndt Hamm, *Promissio, Pactum, Ordinatio: Freiheit und Selbstbindung Gottes in der scholastischen Gnadenlehre* (Tübingen: Mohr Siebeck, 1977).

3. See Oswald Bayer, *Martin Luther's Theology: A Contemporary Interpretation*, trans. Thomas H. Trapp (Grand Rapids: Eerdmans, 2008), pp. 40-67.

4. See Bo Kristian Holm and Peter Widmann, eds., *Word-Gift-Being: Justification-Economy-Ontology* (Tübingen: Mohr Siebeck, 2009), pp. 195-206 for bibliography. Three other

Without writing a full history of promise, we may indicate some decisive moments. Promise emerged in modern theology only after a long period of retrieval and development. Although the recovery of biblical eschatology in the work of Johannes Weiss and Albert Schweitzer did not put forward promise as a decisive concept, it paved the way for the explicit attention to promise in interpretation of Martin Luther's early exegetical writing. Promise emerged clearly and decisively in these writings and their exegesis by Karl Holl, the members of the Luther Renaissance, and the host of German and Scandinavian theologians who engaged the early Luther in the Weimar Era and beyond.[5] In this, the name of Hans-Joachim Iwand is especially important.[6] Oswald Bayer revolutionized the study of Luther by his retrieval and examination of promise.[7] Promise continues to play a significant role in his work.[8] In the latter twentieth century, promise has played a significant and crucial role in developing the midcentury eschatologically-driven theologies of Wolfhart Pannenberg, Jürgen Moltmann, and Robert W. Jenson.[9] All of these theologians use promise in various ways and all have a played an important role in raising the question of promise, how to consider it in theology, and what its role is for practice.

Among these contributors to promise's return to theology in the twentieth century, Bayer has pointed the way forward through his articulation of promise as a "categorical gift."[10] This insight and connection provides the

recent contributions are Hans Christian Knuth, ed., *Angeklagt und Anerkannt: Luthers Rechtfertigungslehre in gegenwärtiger Verantwortung* (Erlangen: Martin-Luther-Verlag, 2009); Veronika Hoffmann, ed., *Die Gabe: Ein "Urwort" der Theologie?* (Frankfurt: Verlag Otto Lembeck, 2009); Jan-Olav Henrikson, *Desire, Gift, and Recognition: Christology and Postmodern Philosophy* (Grand Rapids: Eerdmans, 2009).

5. Gregory Walter, "Karl Holl (1866-1926) and the Recovery of Promise in Luther," *Lutheran Quarterly* 25 (2011): 398-413.

6. Gregory Walter, "An Introduction to Hans Joachim Iwand's *The Righteousness of Faith According to Luther*," *Lutheran Quarterly* 21 (2007): 17-26.

7. Oswald Bayer, *Promissio: Geschichte der reformatischen Wende in Luthers Theologie*, 2nd ed. (Darmstadt: Wissenschaftliche Buchgesellschaft, 1989).

8. Oswald Bayer, *Theologie* (Gütersloh: Gütersloher Verlagshaus, 1994).

9. I offer here only the works that decisively discuss promise: Wolfhart Pannenberg, "Dogmatische Thesen zur Lehre von der Offenbarung," in *Offenbarung als Geschichte*, ed. Wolfhart Pannenberg (Göttingen: Vandenhoeck & Ruprecht, 1965), pp. 91-114; Jürgen Moltmann, *Theologie der Hoffnung: Untersuchungen zur Begründung und zu den Konsequenzen einer christlichen Eschatologie* (Munich: Chr. Kaiser Verlag, 1965); Robert W. Jenson, *Story and Promise: A Brief Theology of the Gospel* (Philadelphia: Fortress Press, 1973).

10. Oswald Bayer, "Categorical Imperative or Categorical Gift?" in *Freedom in Response: Lutheran Ethics; Sources and Controversies*, trans. Jeffrey F. Cayzer (Oxford: Oxford University Press, 2007), pp. 13-20.

3

starting point for this essay. Outside of Bayer, theologians have only used speech-act to make sense of promise. This insight is decisive, and Bayer takes it in the direction of the beginning of theology. Since gift is a practice, it can aid in the articulation of a post-foundational method for theology.[11] This kind of method has been argued for by each of these theologians in their various ways.

In drastic summary, post-foundationalism involves a recognition that our ways of making theological claims or doctrines cannot proceed as they ordinarily have under the conditions of modernity or, as some argue in a sociological terms, under the canopy of Christendom.[12] This means that theologians have to undertake their reflection, criticism, and construction with a view toward a more limited form of justification, one that allows us to establish the truth of Christian claims and practices on the basis of their success in a pluralist setting. In modernity, it is generally understood that every discourse or practice should be viable only if it can be based upon clear, public, and shared grounds, grounds that are accessible to every person and are immediately or self-evidently true. Such a situation does not obtain in today's world of mind-boggling plurality, if it ever held true in modernity itself. Thus, to attend to the post-foundational tasks of theology one need not only consider this task generated by the prodding of philosophers in the tradition of analytical or continental philosophy.

This situation also is a feature of the social dimensions of the theological enterprise, the state of the world in which theology is practiced. One cannot count on an easy continuity to hold between the world of the church, the world of the academy, and the world of the world. In this state of affairs, Christians can no longer count on a rationality or set of truths common to themselves and others. Rather, this situation of radical plurality demands a different way of making arguments. To simplify the responses to this situation, this means for some that Christians must appeal only to a specifically Christian form of justification, leaving the task of communication to require the rhetorical flexibility to make sense of Christian claims in public. For others, this means a task to somehow take into account this plurality within their

---

11. See, among the vast literature on this subject, Kathryn Tanner, *Theories of Culture: A New Agenda for Theology* (Minneapolis: Fortress Press, 1997), and Graham Ward, *Cultural Transformation and Religious Practice* (Cambridge: Cambridge University Press, 2005).

12. The literature on post-foundational thought and practice is vast. For a summary, see John E. Thiel, *Nonfoundationalism* (Minneapolis: Fortress Press, 2000), as well as J. Wentzel van Huyssteeen, *The Shaping of Rationality: Toward Interdisciplinarity in Theology and Science* (Grand Rapids: Eerdmans, 1999).

schemes of justification, to draw the plurality of the world into the heart of Christian theological practice.

We need not decide between these matters here, since attention to the practice of gift allows for a sense of promise that is open to public and pluralist criticism, leaving open the question of the justification of this project, yet offering a post-foundational and post-metaphysical account of promise as gift. This means that my analysis of the implications of the phenomena of promise requires intelligibility across several domains. In particular, it needs to make sense across the domains of theology and of cultural anthropology, shuttling back and forth between the two in order to flesh out promise. Indeed, we should observe that a post-foundational account recognizes the intertwining of domains of intelligibility and justification such that one cannot draw strict boundaries between theology on the one hand and cultural anthropology, for instance, on the other.[13] This plurality and attention to the singularity of promise requires a post-metaphysical approach to theology since I will highlight several moments where a metaphysical concept of actuality restricts and negates the phenomenon of promise. This means that if promise is to have a successful interpretive category for scripture, theology, and mission, several antecedent conceptions of God's being and power shall need to be set aside.[14]

While my arguments at times make considerable use of cultural anthropological and phenomenological modes of interpretation, such modes are not exhaustive or sufficient to be a full substitute for theology and its own discursive traditions. Nor is phenomenology a necessary pre-theological move, since I offer at many places a correction of the orientation phenomenology can provide. The writers whose work provides important stimulus and helpful concepts in articulating the concept and practice of promise are considerable contributors to the phenomenological tradition. All this is to say that the phenomenological tradition has made significant contributions to hermeneutics, theology of culture, and the gift, and needs to be taken up when considering these matters. But in this book I do not offer an analysis of promise in the full dress of contemporary phenomenology. To do so would severely limit its accessibility as theology and distract from the many impor-

13. Here I follow the view of Robert Scharlemann, "Constructing Theological Models," *Journal of Religion* 53 (1973): 63-82.

14. The revision of theological concepts in light of post-metaphysical and post-foundational thought is well summarized by Calvin O. Schrag, *God as Otherwise Than Being: Toward a Semantics of the Gift* (Evanston: Northwestern University Press, 2002), and John Panteleimon Manoussakis, *God After Metaphysics: A Theological Aesthetic* (Bloomington: Indiana University Press, 2007).

tant vistas opened by God's promise in the crucified Jesus because it would take up questions concerning the possibility of phenomena, the character of interpretation, and the interpreter. This project awaits. Likewise, cultural anthropology offers significant contributions to understanding promise as gift; indeed, my project would be impossible without this body of work. My specific engagement with the limitations for theology of cultural anthropology shall emerge throughout the book itself. These limitations are summarized by their limited applicability to the God of Israel, who promises the impossible.

Finally, a note on the theological scope of this essay: what the Christian tradition calls God's grace may indeed be best understood as promise. It may also be possible to consider God's gracious acts entirely as acts of promise. But this book does not argue for that. To do so would require other sets of considerations, most of all the character of God's creation, the eschatological scope of God's actions, and the interminable question of God's being. Rather than take up these valuable questions, I hope to clarify the phenomenon of promise as gift and to show its theological, hermeneutical, and ethical significance. Throughout this book several arguments for how God can and does promise emerge but they are secondary to the discussion of promise itself.

1.2. Types of Gift

I shall argue that promise is a kind of gift — one that is doubled and extended. This means that a promise consists of two moments of giving, both the pledge and then the actual giving of the promise, with the doubled gift extended over time in between the two. This means that we shall examine the phenomenon of promise in order to show not only how the offering of a promise bears a family resemblance to what anthropologists call gift-exchange or gift-economies but also how promise, theologically considered, escapes or resolves many of the problems that trouble the gift's ingress into theology. The promise is a pure gift that enables reciprocity, in a way, bringing together disparate types of the gift. These types of gift were created by problems in accounting for gifts and the question whether they always carry obligation. These problems stem from the anthropologist's constant reminder that all gifts have strings attached to them or the phenomenologist's analysis that the gift, freed from all of obligation, a truly free gift, is utterly impossible. These problems have led theologians to champion some kinds of gifts over others. Before examining these problems, we need to take up the gift briefly and outline the kinds of gifts cultural anthropologists have described.

Gifts are, according to anthropologists, highly symbolic and public acts that create, efface, or distort social relationships.[15] Though they are gifts of material objects that can relieve material needs such as hunger, poverty, and want, they also have social functions, meaning they create, alter, and shape communal and social identity. They draw the boundaries of communities and they welcome strangers. To receive a gift means taking on a particular social role, taking up the challenge to give in return, or similar social dynamics. Fieldwork in Melanesia and the Pacific Northwest initiated discussion of the gift in cultural anthropology, and the gift has been observed throughout antiquity and, albeit in other guises, in contemporary life. Wherever there are social practices, the gift lurks somewhere in the backdrop as its schema. Activities such as forgiveness and hospitality can be construed as forms of gift-exchange.[16]

Ever since the gift started attracting the attention of cultural theorists and philosophers, theologians have also sifted through the legacy of the gift to consider its benefits for Christian doctrine, liturgy, and ethics. Following Marcel Mauss, analysis of the gift lies at the heart of many different theories of human society.[17] Though many in this line, along with Mauss, have considered the possibilities of a gift-economy replacing or somehow remedying the travails of a capital-economy, interest in the gift for theological purposes extends into other practices and theoretical problems. Promise belongs to the soil of gift-exchange.

My chief discussion partners in this book are Marcel Mauss and Jacques Derrida. Mauss, a pioneering cultural anthropologist, initiated discussion of the gift. He is the great patron of this whole discourse on the gift; following the work of Bronislaw Malinowski, Mauss outlined the basic scheme of the gift. Gift-exchange occurs as a public act that creates three obligations: to give, to receive, and to return the gift.[18] Each of the subsequent chapters will take up a dimension of Mauss's three obligations in order to show how promise is an extended and doubled gift. Jacques Derrida, a philosopher, advocates the impossible gift, the pure gift that carries no obligation. His insistence that the conditions of the gift in Mauss's sense in fact make the pure gift impossible presents an important challenge for theology to consider.

15. Maurice Godelier, *The Enigma of Gift*, trans. Nora Scott (Chicago: University of Chicago Press, 1999), pp. 10-42.

16. Karen Margaret Sykes, *Arguing with Anthropology: An Introduction to Critical Theories of the Gift* (London: Routledge, 2005).

17. Marcel Mauss, *The Gift: The Form and Reason for Exchange in Archaic Society*, trans. W. D. Halls (New York: Norton, 1990).

18. Mauss, *The Gift*, p. 13.

The long history of reflection on gift-exchange has developed several different accounts of why gifts are given and the obligations involved, none of them completely unproblematic. The first kind of gift is the pure, unilateral, or free gift. From the start, Malinowski and Mauss disagreed on whether gifts are owed instead of being freely offered, with Malinowski finally acquiescing to Mauss. Malinowski called gifts that have no obligation "pure gifts."[19] Such a gift also can be referred to as "free," in the negative sense that the gift does not have any strings attached to it. Derrida and Jean-Luc Marion advocate this pure gift.

The other major type of gift is the archaic, reciprocated gift. This gift, the gift that is governed by obligation, sent in a circle, is the only gift that Mauss considered to exist. We shall use these various ways of articulating the gift in understanding promise as gift. But first, we shall take up the speech-act theoretical analysis of promise.

Between the pure and archaic gifts we find two middling sorts of gifts. Closer to the pure gift is Kathryn Tanner's "unconditional" gift, which attempts to remove all reciprocity, the need to give back and forth, yet maintain some form of obligation.[20] Likewise, John Milbank advocates a "purified gift," which is the archaic gift that is exchanged, upholds reciprocity, but eschews the agonistic and violent elements that intrude in Mauss's model.[21] Paul Ricoeur also argues for something like the purified gift when he advocates that participants in gift-exchange distinguish good and injurious reciprocity.

Of particular importance to the gift is the way that all of these authors have considered it as a means of creating, altering, and severing social relationships and community. One gives gifts for the purpose of dominating others just as much as to demonstrate equality by showing that one can match another's ability to give. Since gift-exchange is embedded in a wide variety of human practices and social relations, many practices such as forgiveness or hospitality could in fact carry with them hidden obligations or a force of domination and mastery. What is common to all of these acts is the frequent observation of writers on the gift: that the language for the gift itself shows that it could at once be benefit and poison. The word for gift in many languages has held this dual meaning.[22]

In summary, to take up promise as gift will be a way to theologically dis-

19. Bronislaw Malinowski, *Argonauts of the Western Pacific* (New York: Dutton, 1953), p. 177.

20. Kathryn Tanner, *Economy of Grace* (Minneapolis: Fortress Press, 2005), pp. 63-72.

21. John Milbank, "Can a Gift Be Given? Prolegomena to a Future Trinitarian Metaphysics," *Modern Theology* 11 (1995): 119-59.

22. Emile Benveniste, *Indo-European Language and Society*, trans. Elizabeth Palmer (Coral Gables: University of Miami Press, 1973), pp. 53-98.

cuss social practice, obligation, and human action just as much as to consider its significance for the theological task of interpreting, constructing, and communicating Christian claims.

1.3. Speech-Acts and Promise

Long before the adoption of the anthropological category of practices became widespread in theological discourse, promise played a significant role in the development of speech-acts by J. L. Austin and his successors.[23] Though the speech-act does make sense of the matter of promise, it does not entirely suffice to account for the promise since the speech-act trains its energies only on the initial act of making a promise. This inadequacy comes, in part, from attempts by Austin and others to purify speech-act theory and partially from the phenomenon of promise that theorists try to describe. Speech-act theory is important because it shows that words do things and have force beyond referring to other realities. Problems emerge when theorists try to purify and specify exactly how and what that force entails. This produces a need to utilize other resources such as those of gift-exchange that I put forward in this book in an attempt to develop both the descriptive and normative contours of a theological account of promise.

Austin took the promise as the main example of a performative, a use of words to do something, to undertake or produce an event, instead of the more common use of language to claim or to refer, which he initially categorizes as a constative act.[24] This dominant method for considering promise has had significance for several major theological proposals and remains at the core of many philosophical and theological projects.[25]

Theologians use speech-act theory to take into account the force of a promise and to claim that theology proceeds from promise as a speech-act to move beyond the problems of verification, falsification, if not beyond the problems of true and false propositions.[26] This seems to provide the way for-

---

23. Of lesser significance is the *Sprachereignis* developed by Ernst Fuchs and Gerhard Ebeling. This specific hermeneutical theology has been applied to promise that largely proves inadequate. See also the criticism of speech-event by Christopher Morse, *The Logic of Promise in Moltmann's Theology* (Philadelphia: Fortress Press, 1979), pp. 49-52.

24. J. L. Austin, *How to Do Things with Words,* ed. J. O. Urmson and Marina Sbisà, 2nd ed. (Cambridge: Harvard University Press, 1975), p. 3.

25. Richard J. Bernstein outlines the long influence of the role of speech-act and practice in Anglo-American philosophy in *Beyond Objectivism and Relativism: Science, Hermeneutics, and Praxis* (Philadelphia: University of Pennsylvania Press, 1988), pp. 109-15.

26. See Oswald Bayer, *Theologie* (Gütersloh: Gütersloher Verlagshaus, 1994), pp. 487-

ward for theologians to articulate theology without the need to ground their propositions in a modern or foundationalist sense. Foundationalism in this context means the demand for a practitioner in a discipline to ground, justify, or enable their discourse with reference to indubitable or clear and public propositions. Thus, these grounding claims provide, in this architectural metaphor, the foundation for building the discourse. Speech-acts seem to open up space for a post-foundational approach, which means that theologians have the promise and may clearly proceed from it to delimit the scope, nature, and purpose of theology. Rather than having to appeal to experience or only that which can be justified by appeal to empirical evidence of the sort demanded by the social or natural sciences, theologians have sought refuge in non-foundationalism in order to justify or enable their enterprise. If speech-acts do something instead of claiming, referring, or stating a proposition that can be falsified or verified, then they seem to fund theologians who wish to proceed without foundations if theology emerges from the event of a performance rather than from a claim.

But speech-acts are not pure; the force they effect cannot be delimited or circumscribed by their circumstances or conventions. There have been attempts to purify speech-acts and give them a clear set of rules that circumscribe the act of promising, shoring up the activity so that we can, in the initial act, decide that this is in fact a successful promise and that one is not. This delimitation of promise by certain rules or conventions exorcises the risk of promise, the fact that its failure is a condition of promising. Austin and John Searle frequently idealize promise as if they could develop rules or conditions that, if met, would show how a promise would go off properly and be carried to its conclusion. Austin considers failed promises to be parasitical and secondary to the pure promise, the one that succeeds and is worthy of the name.[27] But, since, in the case of promise, the time involved, its doubling and repetition, does not permit us to say that a promise can be reduced entirely to the initial act, it lies in the future. Since a promise extends onward, the speech-act only concerns the promise's initial moment, the words or form followed by the promiser that are established by the circumstances or context that surrounds the speech-act and the conventions that sustain the form of the promise, the quasi-ritual that one follows to make a promise. Austin wants to avoid the reduction of promise to the inward intention and disposition of the one promising. He holds that this lets perjurers off the hook because they say one thing

99. Reinhard Hütter offers significant criticism of this approach in *Suffering Divine Things: Theology as Church Practice*, trans. Doug Stott (Grand Rapids: Eerdmans, 1997), pp. 77-86.

27. J. L. Austin, *How to Do Things with Words*, pp. 12-24.

and mean another. He aims to find a way to make promises stick, to hold the promisor to account by maintaining that the outward form binds the inward intention. Nevertheless, the promiser's intention matters since it helps to shore up the ambiguity that promises introduce. Questions and qualifications multiply that make us doubt that any promise worthy of the name has ever appeared. Shall a promise prove to be "false"? Does the promiser have the ability to make the promise happen? To be sure, Austin holds that this failure is an infelicity. Since the internal disposition of the promiser is unavailable, no one may determine whether the promise is properly offered until its end. What this points out, Derrida argues, is that the conditions for making a promise succeed actually make it impossible. This is all not to say that there are no promises, just that there are no pure promises, a problem similar to that of the pure gift. If a gift may appear that is pure of all obligations, how can it be if it is recognized by the giver, seen as a gift, and accepted by the recipient? In each case, the gift appears as such and so registers itself on the consciousness of the participants, showing itself and therefore the relationships established by the gift, its history, and the obligations that attend it. Even if one gives anonymously, there remains a giver and so a need for return. The conditions of the gift, writes Derrida, make the gift impossible.

Derrida shows how the problem of the speech-act is similar to the problem of the gift. The first of these is the most serious, which involves the very definition of a promise that is at odds with itself. Derrida writes, "In order to be a promise, a promise must be able to be broken and therefore be able not to be a promise (for a breakable promise is not a promise). Conclusion: one will never state, any more than for the gift, that there is or that there has been a promise."[28] This means that a promise necessarily includes its failure in it. This undoes the promise.

Derrida articulated these difficulties, difficulties that demonstrate the need for another way to consider promise.[29] These problems all have a com-

28. Jacques Derrida, "Avances," in Serge Margel, *Le tombeau du Dieu artisan: Sur Platon* (Paris: Minuit, 1995), p. 26.

29. Derrida mainly criticized Austin on the ability of the theorist to properly delimit the rules and context of the speech-act, to shore up a situation saturated with contexts, contexts multiplied beyond count. Likewise, if promise depends upon certain circumstances, that is, one requires conventions to be able to identify when a promise is being made, it is impossible to draw the context tightly enough for a promise to be isolated since the meaning of the force of the speech-act always disseminates beyond and within the hearers and cannot be reduced to the intention of the speaker nor the forms that observers like the speech-act theorist draw. See Jacques Derrida, "Signature Event Context," in *Limited, Inc.,* trans. Samuel Weber and Jeffrey Mehlman (Evanston: Northwestern University Press, 1988), pp. 1-24.

mon root that Derrida claims to find in Austin: Austin's intention that clear and distinct rules obtain for speech-acts such that we can have a clear instance of promise before us. Derrida does not reject speech-acts entirely but claims they are always a bit off and always fall short. Derrida's way of finding the impure speech-act is to blur the clear and solid distinctions between intention and act or to eliminate boundaries around the context or circumstances of the speech-act. This is a revision, not a rejection of speech-act theory as follows. A speech-act is still a way that words have force:

> By no means do I draw the conclusion that there is no relative specificity of effects of consciousness or of effects of speech . . . that there is no performative event [speech-act]. It is simply that those effects do not exclude what is generally opposed to them, term by term; on the contrary, they presuppose it, in an asymmetrical way, as the general space of their possibility.[30]

For the purposes of this book, this means that a speech-act includes its failures. This means that from the perspective of speech-act theory there are no pure promises, no promises that succeed in their entirety when viewed from their initial pledge. In order to take up a promise we must attend to its extension, that it is an event that extends over time as much as it is an initial act or its final arrival. We gather from a chastened speech-act theory that the words of promise have force, and the force they have is of a gift.

The difficulties facing promise expand, similar to the gift. A promise is structurally similar to a threat. Both of them involve an initial pledge and the time that lapses between the pledge/threat and its fulfillment. Threats, as we learn, can be credible. So can promises. This means that we need time and must await the conclusion of the threat or promise to determine its danger or longing welcome. Thus, a promise is of itself opened up to dispute and disbelief if it is indeed a promise and so credible.

1.4. Plan of the Book

Mauss outlines the gift in terms of three obligations: one is obliged to give, to receive, and to offer a counter-gift in return. These three obligations occur over time and require an indeterminate but appropriate delay between each turn in the gift-cycle. Promise is a doubled and extended gift. It is a weak

---

30. Derrida, "Signature Event Context," p. 19.

power that gives a possibility directed toward the neighbor. It is open to public criticism and evaluation. Promise occupies no place and gives the place of the neighbor, requiring a radical kind of hospitality. Each of these claims can be taken up according to the elements of gift that Mauss sketches. I have organized the analysis of promise as gift by following these three obligations and the time between them, additionally considering the place of the gift, a subject to which Mauss does not explicitly attend.

Therefore, in the second chapter I will provide much of the groundwork for a consideration of promise as gift and its particular obligation. I will uncover the phenomenon of promise by considering the Hospitality of Sarah and Abraham (Gen. 18:1-15). Following that, I shall consider the power, being, and time of the promise by an analysis of the Icon of Pentecost in the third chapter. This emerges from an account of the delay involved in promise. In the fourth chapter I will take up the obligation to receive and return the gift, showing how the promise enables a kind of impure giving, which is to show how the promise interacts with the plurality of life and the many ways that God acts with and beyond the promise. And finally, the fifth chapter will show the place of the promise and the community it engenders.

CHAPTER 2

Promise as Gift

> *Sarah's laughter's sudden, like a hurdle, like an old loud crow*
> *that comes out of the blue.*
> *The graceful men at the makeshift table —*
> *there, in the shade of the tree, in the heat of the day, in Bethel —*
> *look up from the all too tender veal,*
> *the buttermilk, the three small*
> *cakes of meal she's made them. For her husband*
> *Abraham, she's sifted, shaped them in her old dry hand.*

Gillian Allnutt, "Sarah's Laughter"

Sarah's laughter gives us promise; her rejection of the blessing offered by the strangers at Mamre combines her longing for and rejection of the impossible that they offer. In her laughter, she brings together the contrary movements of the biblical narrative that will allow us to discover promise as gift.

In taking up this text, this chapter will present the practice and concept of promise as a doubled and extended gift; it will show that promise interacts with, transforms, and interrupts gift economies in a way that will address a basic impasse between rival conceptions of the obligation involved in gifts; it will further show that any treatment of promise needs to attend to the relationship between this promise as gift and being, a relationship that will show that God's act of promise elevates possibility over actuality. In addition to its more strictly theological importance, the exchange of gifts raises ethical questions, particularly the question of power and gift put this way: whether human beings, nature, or God can ever give freely or whether they always have some obligation that they bear, demanding return. This question haunts discussion of the gift, warning theologians who would make use of discussions of the gift as well as serving as the major challenge to taking up the gift in practice.

The basic contours of the phenomenon of promise emerge through an interpretation of the Hospitality of Abraham and Sarah (Gen. 18:1-15). The promise, as we shall see, is a kind of gift that is exchanged, invites a response, yet remains free of all obligations. It differs from the kinds of gift that circulate or preserve themselves absolutely from any obligation while sharing in them all. We will examine in this chapter the concept of promise as a gift, indicating the areas of investigation that we will further pursue.

The legacy of anthropological and philosophical discussion of gifts has issued a fairly stable set of categories. Gifts can be described geometrically as circles or vectors, organizing the crucial categories of time, obligation, and action. Emmanuel Levinas distinguished between the circular travel of Odysseus and the open path of Abraham.[1] Odysseus wandered but always was returning home. Abraham, by contrast, left his home to follow YHWH. These two figures represent the archaic and the pure gift, also known as the reciprocal and the unilateral gift.

Odysseus, though traveling through many places and lands, still pressed toward his home. He sought to return from whence he came. He sought to repeat and return to what was before. This figure can be taken to be the gift that travels in a circle, seeks to return, and carries with it obligation. Marcel Mauss discusses this in terms of the "spirit" of the gift; gifts always seek their origin, they always "come back" to the original giver in some fashion, hence the similar description of this gift as a reciprocal gift, one that involves a return, a counter-gift from the recipient after a certain delay of time has passed. Jacques Derrida summarizes the exchange and return of gifts, what he calls an economy, as circular.[2] The agonistic or archaic gift is the gift that can be either violent or peaceful. It can seek equilibrium where justice exists, yet it demands a counter-gift. Some thinkers further assimilate the figure of Odysseus to that of love as eros, which some define as the fulfillment of desire and the seeking of the same. Finally, the archaic and circular gift is furthered by three obligations: one must give, must receive, and must return. These obligations, however motivated, ensure that the gift follows a circular path to its origin.

By contrast, Abraham represents the unilateral and pure gift; he strikes

---

1. Emmanuel Levinas, "Le trace d'Autre," *Tijdschrift voor filosofie* 25 (1963): 610.

2. Jacques Derrida, *Given Time: 1. Counterfeit Money,* trans. Peggy Kamuf (Chicago: University of Chicago Press, 1992), pp. 7-8.

out from the known into the unknown, from the old into the new. He does not remain tied to Ur, to his homeland. Instead, he seeks out new places. This gift is pure and does not demand any return to origins. It strikes out on its own, scattering and disseminating itself without any return. It is a dispersal of leaves without any gathering up of them again. Time figures differently into the unilateral gift since there is no return needed and so no delay; perhaps the pure gift takes no time at all since it is without strings and obligations. In modernity this kind of gift has been assimilated to the form of love sometimes called agape, the disinterested and selfless love that does not seek its own good but that of an other.

Setting the circle and the vector alongside one another, we can see the task at hand. A promise might seem to be circular, on the one hand, since it involves the promise of one to another, the responsibility and credibility of the one to the other, and so a relationship of reciprocity and the circle. But it is also surprising, chancy, and seems to be unilateral in direction. To speak about promise after the fashion of the geometers here is to state that the promise is both circular and a vector. It brings Odysseus and Abraham into one figure. It points outward, as a vector, while returning.[3] Promise offers a chance to eliminate the false contrast between love as eros and agape. Abraham, therefore, may be said to leave home to find it ever anew elsewhere. And Sarah both rejects and loves the impossible. Together this couple embody promise in the search for a home.

2.1. From Melanesia to Mamre

As the subject of reflective and analytical discussion, the gift started in one sense with Marcel Mauss and his *Essay on the Gift*. His studies of Melanesian society construct the now-classic account of the archaic or agonistic gift. He makes high claims for this gift, its decisive role in the life of archaic societies, and its limping, marginal survival in modern culture. He describes it as a bond for human community and the motor that weaves together things and persons into a culture. These connections are the crucial matter that arose from early anthropological study of the gift. Mauss sifts through data from many different cultures, ancient and contemporary, to summarize a crucial dimension of gift economy: that agency can be attributed to things that are given and that people can be treated like things because of the way gifts circu-

---

3. John Milbank has made a similar comparison in his essay "Can a Gift Be Given? Prolegomena to a Future Trinitarian Metaphysics," *Modern Theology* 11 (1995): 160n.76.

late. He observes this in the gift-exchanges practiced in two different rituals: the Melanesian kula ring and the Pacific Northwestern potlatch. As different as these ceremonies are, Mauss finds in them the pattern of the archaic gift that cuts across their respective cultures. He writes, "What imposes obligation in the present received and exchanged is the fact that the thing received is not inactive. Even when it has been abandoned by the giver, it still possesses something of him."[4] Thus, a gift and its donor are connected; the recipient gains a relationship with the donor through the medium of the gift; the gift itself constitutes the relationship. Mauss considers these connections to be established by the gift itself. This requires him to argue that gifts have agency, possessed by a spirit, called *hau*. These theses form Mauss's summary of archaic gift-exchange as a total social fact — the web of relationships that make a society is a web made up of gifts and attendant practices.[5]

Without endorsing the Maori view of the *hau* that permeates Mauss's discussion in *The Gift*, we can note that discussion of gift-exchanges requires attention to this ambiguous boundary between gifts and their donors. By this we can extend the use of "gift" to that which appears to us; we can find that gifts therefore have as much to do with nature as with culture. Nature gives in the sense of that which is given to human agents as raw data (the given), for instance, the surprising appearance of good weather for crops. This is what Mauss is getting at when he presents the economy of gift-exchange as a "total social fact." While many dimensions of gift economies — such as hospitality, friendship, and honor — have found their way into theological and philosophical discussions, these discussions have been hampered by a basic impasse that has attended reflection on the gift since Mauss: gifts seem to be either unilateral or reciprocal. On the one hand, we cherish the idea that gifts come without any obligation; yet we worry about their effect, their legacy, and what is owed to the donor. We recognize that a gift could be unwelcome and coercive. These everyday concerns relate to the complex matters of the force of this obligation, the character of reciprocity.

The result of defining gifts as practices that either are unilateral or reciprocal, as Mauss argues, opposes this use of "give" in everyday language as well as the expectation of what gifts are. Many social and religious understandings of gifts in contemporary culture define them as freely given, coming without obligations; perhaps anonymously offered or highly personal, fa-

---

4. Marcel Mauss, *The Gift: The Form and Reason for Exchange in Archaic Society*, trans. W. D. Halls (New York: Norton, 1990), p. 12. Mauss invoked the Maori concept of the *hau* as part of the explanation of why obligation attends gifts.

5. Mauss called it a "total social fact" that weaves together the wide variety of social phenomena; *The Gift*, pp. 13-14.

milial, and intimate in character; and always unmerited. These social and religious traditions deem it important to construe gifts as free; Mauss shocks discussion of gift-giving by claiming that all gifts belong to a ring of exchange. He alerts us to the archaic features of the gift: that it involves obligation, occurs publicly, and takes time.

In this circle, gifts are not free; one has an obligation to give, accept, and return them. The figure of the circle, as Derrida notes, is a figure appropriate to the flow of a gift whose exchange establishes and maintains relations between donors and recipients. Indeed, Mauss describes the kula exchange as a ring that connects all the various tribes of the Trobriand Islands. His compilation of anthropological data shows that gifts and the larger gift economy belong to a matter of obligation and are not free. Freedom intrudes only when one wishes to interrupt the circle of giving in a negative fashion. Such a sundering of the bonds is a gesture of violence and war.[6]

Most of Mauss's legatees dispute elements of his picture of the archaic gift. Some want to change his explanation of the exchange of gifts, the reasons why obligations obtain, and why the gift must be accepted and returned. On these mainly anthropological grounds, some claim Mauss does not properly account for why the gift must return. We will take up the counter-gift and reciprocity in a later chapter. Other readers of Mauss's work take a different tack. Chief among these is Derrida, whose reflections on the gift count for us the second major stage in this study, since he introduces an understanding of the gift as a unilateral and pure gift, a gift that has no strings attached; he holds to this gift, hopes after its existence not only for ethical and political reasons but also for phenomenological reasons. For Derrida, discussion of the gift is part and parcel of the question of what is, what exists, what being is and is not, because the gift is part of what is given. Derrida puts his finger on the question of the gift, for in it he has found a way to talk about being in a post-metaphysical way. Derrida holds that the conditions for the gift are also its annulment. If we are to seek out the pure gift we must tread lightly. He demands high costs for this gift's purity: it must carry with it no demand and no recognition. As an absolute surprise or chance event, this pure gift interrupts any ordinary economy and, once recognized as a gift, dissolves.[7] The pure gift demands a radical forgetfulness because if giver or recipient remembered it, they would be caught in the web of exchange and obligation.[8] His view of the pure gift is one that escapes or is somehow oblique to the economy of gift, of

6. Mauss, *The Gift*, p. 37.
7. Derrida, *Given Time*, pp. 12-14.
8. Derrida, *Given Time*, pp. 16-17.

its reciprocity, cycles, and returns. If promise is a gift, we must think how it might be pure in the sense Derrida articulates.

Mauss's first stage of the anthropological discussion of gift creates a serious challenge not only for any construal of God's giving, if the conceptuality to think God's giving is raised from human giving, but also for the claim made generally in Christian doctrine that God's grace is free. If God were a partner in this circle, wholly encompassed by it, God's giving would compete with human gifts. God would be a giver who dominates, a patron whose gifts would drown their recipients. Such a cycle would constrain God into the field of cause and effect called metaphysics. It would mean that God's agency is constricted by those immanent possibilities. Many times Christians have described God as a patron in this sense, demanding homage, honor, and glory from God's legatees, the world. Additionally, theologians concerned with God's freedom, action, power, or transcendence should likewise worry that ascribing the archaic gift to God's giving would put significant strictures on that freedom, power, action, and transcendence. This brief characterization of God as giver demands attention to such matters as God's freedom or transcendence — matters usually associated with theological ontology, not with human practices. In order to fulfill the post-metaphysical task of theology, we must identify not only those locations where gift-discourses impinge on the doctrines and concepts that theology must articulate, but also where those discourses embrace an all-too-metaphysical construal of reality.

However, we cannot begin to think of God as a promiser without first considering the phenomenon of promise. To take up this task, we must first note that gift represents as a category or name that collects many phenomena under it. Since the nature, significance, and protocol for gift exchange all vary considerably, Mauss schematizes the gift only in the most general terms, or as "a fragment of more general studies."[9] Mauss's heirs extended his studies to include marriage, friendship, and many other practices within the scope of a gift economy. For our purposes, we will attend to hospitality and gift exchange since we will consider the hospitality offered at the oaks of Mamre as our way to think of promise as gift.

The Hospitality of Abraham and Sarah (Gen. 18:1-15) offers a narrative in which we can distinguish a promise from other gifts as a doubled and extended gift. This remarkable scene from Genesis calls for a reconsideration of theological ontology if God promises in this fashion and does not merely give; God's interactions with creation and indeed Godself require closer examination since the action involved in promising draws attention to the be-

9. Mauss, *The Gift*, p. 3.

ing of the agent. Such ontology offers a way to mediate the dispute about the reciprocated gift and its freedom and the difficulties faced by theological adoption of anthropological and philosophical discussion of the gift.

I contend that the promise embraces both the reciprocal gift as well as the gift purified of all exchange and obligation, a gift that is unilateral in its direction yet returns to embrace the circle that it enters. Promise can do this because it is a doubled and extended gift. Yet it seems that these two forms of the gift offer little to the theologian. The first is, of course, the many variations on the archaic gift that survives to this day in vastly altered forms.[10] It seems to bring God into the ordinary give-and-take of human life. The second can interrupt, but almost without sustained effect, always entering into the ordinary like lightning that instantly retreats to the sky. Yet if we consider promise as a gift, we can see how it, as a phenomenon, can interrupt with effect, can engage the ordinary give-and-take without indebting its recipients. In short, it is both the gift-without-strings and the gift that criticizes and transforms the ordinary cycles of life.

So let us proceed. A promise is a kind of gift. If this is the case, gifts must be distinguishable as such but also in kinds. This requires attention to the nature of gifts in general and the possibility of examining a gift. This requires some consideration of the anthropological and philosophical study of the gift — particularly that of Mauss and the use made of his work by philosophers such as Derrida and Jean-Luc Marion, since they have proposed the conditions of the gift. These thinkers demonstrate either the gift's absorption into motions of offering, reception, and return (the kula ring); or else mark it as an-economic — Derrida's term for the pure gift — and outside any circle of gifts.[11] These are gifts that are "crossed out," erased from consciousness in order to preserve their purity, marked by the force they lack as they refuse to enter into the rings of exchange. Derrida claims the gift — if there is any, as he frequently repeats — may be sensed only by its trace or wisps of smoke.[12] This metaphor works well to describe the pure gift, since it is nearly intangi-

---

10. For an account of some of the variety of modern practices that continue the gift, see Jacques T. Goudbout and Alain Caillé, *The World of the Gift,* trans. Donald Winkler (Montreal and Kingston: McGill-Queen's University Press, 1998), and Lewis Hyde, *The Gift: Imagination and the Erotic Life of Property* (New York: Vintage, 1983).

11. "If the figure of the circle is essential to economics, the gift must remain *aneconomic.* Not that it remains foreign to the circle, but it must keep a relation of foreignness to the circle, a relation without relation of familiar foreignness." Derrida, *Given Time,* p. 19.

12. Derrida argued that this occurs through the excess that begins Charles Baudelaire's "Counterfeit Money." The two friends leave a smoking shop with change, so he argues that the incipit of the narrative is smoke and excess. See Derrida, *Given Time,* p. 115.

ble, cannot be grasped and brought to heel, yet it can always be sensed and can leave a trace or mark.

Promises are both more and less fragile than this pure gift. They are more fragile since they rely not only on the intention to give but also on the trust of the receiver. They are sturdier than the pure gift because they can enter into the exchange of gifts and do not need to be preserved from it. A promise doubles itself into the initial pledge and subsequent fulfillment; this first pledge is not the gift itself and so lacks even the standing of an ordinary gift. It is the weakest of phenomena, as we shall see. But it is also stronger since if the recipient of a promise trusts it, there is reality to it and so it acquires body without fully divesting itself into the circle of exchange. A promise always retains a critical reserve that allows for it to interrupt and transform the archaic gift. But it only obtains this substantial weight and presence if it is trusted by the one promise, as we shall see. Within the reality of this extended gift we call a promise, contestable as it is due to the doubling of the promise into an initial pledge and the final gift, recipients and donors can engage the ordinary give-and-take of the gift economy.

2.2. The Strangers' Promise

In order to obtain access to the phenomenon of promise and to consider its relationship to the gift, no better text presents itself to us than the scene of hospitality by the oaks of Mamre. Despite the complex relationship between ancient and modern cosmopolitanism and the practice of hospitality, having recourse to the study of ancient forms of hospitality will help us to consider the interactions of the strangers at Mamre.

We must be careful not to simply map Derrida's reflections on the gift onto the story of Abraham and Sarah's hospitality. Derrida's two major reflections on the gift occur primarily in the context of thinking through Baudelaire's prose poem "Counterfeit Money," a prose poem whose focus is on the interaction of the gift and capital economies. Abraham and Sarah's hospitality is far from modern economies of tobacco, capital, and the figure of the beggar in Baudelaire's writing. Therefore we need to investigate this scene of hospitality in ways that distinguish ancient hospitality from modern notions of cosmopolitanism. Such an inquiry will develop the purpose and significance of Abraham's act, Sarah's laughter, and the promise offered by the three strangers.[13]

---

13. One could also extend this discussion to include the practice of hospitality in the first century. On this, see Bruce J. Malina, "The Received View and What It Cannot Do: III John and

Hospitality in Abraham's world is not remarkable even if it had an element of danger or risk. Seen in the light of Julian Pitt-Rivers's "The Law of Hospitality," Abraham undertakes nothing extraordinary in this text, since if he had considered them true strangers, Abraham would have simply denied hospitality to the men.[14] If the strangers were in fact the other, aliens in an absolute sense, this story would be the site of a radical gift, a gift purified of any exchange. Yet here hospitality is not offered in the radical fashion that Levinas or Derrida consider.[15] The radical gift is fundamentally different from ancient economies of household; if we were pursuing hospitality at length instead of promise, we would need to return to this topic after attending to the unfamiliar and distant in this ancient practice. Levinas and Derrida open up a wide range of important questions for theology and ethics, especially in light of the difficult question of human community and solidarity in the present age. But that important effort would detract from the need to show how the Hospitality of Abraham and Sarah distinguishes itself in what the strangers give to their hosts.

So far as we can determine from the evidence, hospitality was actually only offered to a small range of individuals in the social world of the ancient Near East. The visitors who appear and are welcomed are not strangers so foreign they share nothing in common with Abraham and his household; in offering them hospitality, Abraham takes the strangers as potential or fictive kin. In doing this, Abraham does not exhibit any an-economic gesture toward the strangers. This is not to claim that his hospitality lacks all risk. On the contrary, all such exchanges have some attendant challenge to them. Protocols must be followed in order for honor to be won and for offense, if not open conflict, to be avoided. And it is in this ordinary exchange that we may find the strange in the concluding moments of this text: the guests disturb the narrative by their strange promise.

According to Pitt-Rivers and Victor Matthews, hospitality follows a structure or economy that the Genesis narrative displays perfectly.[16] Despite

Hospitality," *Semeia* 35 (1986): 171-86. For constructive and contemporary theologies of hospitality, see Patrick R. Keifert, *Welcoming the Stranger: A Public Theology of Worship and Evangelism* (Minneapolis: Fortress Press, 1992), and Christine D. Pohl, *Making Room: Recovering Hospitality as a Christian Tradition* (Grand Rapids: Eerdmans, 1999).

14. T. R. Hobbs, "Hospitality in the First Testament and the 'Teleological Fallacy,'" *Journal for the Study of the Old Testament* 95 (2001): 3-30.

15. Jacques Derrida and Anne Dufourmantelle, *On Hospitality: Anne Dufourmantelle Invites Jacques Derrida to Respond*, trans. Rachel Bowlby (Stanford: Stanford University Press, 2000).

16. Julian Pitt-Rivers, "The Law of Hospitality," in *The Fate of Shechem, or the Politics of*

variations in their accounts of the protocols of hospitality, such as what counts as an appropriate gesture by the host and what does not, most scholars agree on the general form that this hospitality takes. It is a practice employed in order to defuse any potential conflict from a stranger passing through:

> The law of hospitality is founded upon ambivalence. It imposes order through an appeal to the sacred, makes the unknown knowable, and replaces conflict by reciprocal honor. It does not eliminate the conflict altogether but places it in abeyance and prohibits its expression. . . . Host and guest must pay each other honor. The host requests the honor of the guest's company — (and this is not merely a self-effacing formula: he gains honor through the number and quality of his guests). The guest is honored by the invitation. . . . To this extent the relationship is reciprocal. But this reciprocity does not obscure the distinction between the roles.[17]

Some groups would never be permitted hospitality, such as trading caravans or military expeditions.[18] So the range and space of hospitality is important — there is a limited zone from which Abraham offers hospitality. The narrative presents this well, beginning the scene when Abraham looks up and sees the three by the oaks of Mamre (v. 1).[19]

Many interpreters, ancient and contemporary, have been attentive to the hospitality that permeates this narrative, drawing attention to various dimensions of the story.[20] The actions of Abraham and Sarah, both practitioners of the nomadic life, would have raised for their readers the problems of hospitality. They are obligated to receive the strangers. Their efforts to offer respite to the strangers the wilderness bears them fit into the laws of Mauss's archaic gift. It offers something to another and so it demands a counter-gift in return. Hospitality is reciprocated.

Abraham's hospitality thus demands a counter-gift. Hospitality affords space, time, and sustenance to another. What the strangers offer Sarah and

---

Sex: Essays in the Anthropology of the Mediterranean (Cambridge: Cambridge University Press, 1977), pp. 107-12; Victor H. Matthews and Don C. Benjamin, "The Host and the Stranger," in *The Social World of Ancient Israel, 1250-587 BCE* (Peabody: Hendrickson, 1993), pp. 83-85.

17. Pitt-Rivers, "The Law of Hospitality," p. 107.

18. Hobbs, "Hospitality in the First Testament," pp. 17-18.

19. Parenthetical citations refer to verses in Genesis 18.

20. For this overview of ancient and modern commentary, see Andrew E. Arterbury, "Abraham's Hospitality among Jewish and Early Christian Writers," *Perspectives in Religious Studies* 30 (2006): 359-76; Claus Westermann, *Genesis: 12–36*, trans. John J. Sullion, S.J. (Minneapolis: Fortress Press, 1995), pp. 272-82; Lars Thunberg, "Early Christian Interpretations of the Three Angels in Gen. 18," *Studia Patristica* 7 (1966): 560-70.

Abraham bears close attention since it affords entry into the phenomenology of promise. Rather than giving a counter-gift in response to the hospitality, an offering that acknowledges that a peace — however temporary — holds between the strangers and the hosts, these three visitors instead offer a promise. This does not constitute a proper counter-gift. It might be nothing at all, an empty promise. The promise of a son to Sarah and Abraham, this offered token, is both less than a gift and more than one.

In order to further substantiate how this offer is the offer of a promise, we must attend to the role of the guest in the practice of ancient hospitality. Matthews notes that an appropriate counter-gift is blessing the host, which may take various forms.[21] The guests give their host honor according to the protocols of hospitality in their local society. They may honor their host with news from abroad, gifts of their own, or a blessing upon the host. Matthews considers it appropriate for the guest to bless the host by speaking well of his progeny. If this were so, this would undo our concept of promise since it would show that the transfer of gifts remains closed within a circle established between guest and host.

What matters most here is to identify how the guests at Mamre upset the economy of hospitality, the careful balance between host and guest. Since hospitality is a temporary arrangement and one practiced in order to defuse potentially dangerous situations, it relies on the establishment of a sort of equality, however fictional, between the host and guest to establish a relationship, as all archaic gifts do. In Pitt-Rivers's model of the protocol, guests must accept what their hosts offer, otherwise they upstage and usurp the hosts of the house. Likewise, the hosts cannot overwhelm the guests for fear of unsettling the fragile peace between hosts and guest, so Abraham minimizes the effort he undertakes to serve the guests (vv. 4-5). So we can see that the offer of hospitality by Abraham does expect some sort of reciprocal gift. Indeed, the strangers appropriately offer a blessing that honors the host and his house. But they give too much. A problem arises when the pledge of a son that they give disturbs Sarah. As Horace writes, "*Multa fidem promissa leuant.*" Lavish promises lessen credit.[22]

Sarah laughs, and her laughter upends the carefully balanced scene of hospitality Abraham has set. In Derrida's language, the guests and the laughter constitute an event. Her disbelief, if we may take her laughter to in part signify such incredulity, is an important point of contention that focuses our attention to the blessing of the strangers. The promise of a son is too much

---

21. Matthews and Benjamin, "The Host and the Stranger," pp. 86-87.
22. Horace, *Epistulae* 2.2.

for Sarah — this indicates that we must more closely consider the nature of their counter-gift, for reciprocate they must. They do not offer the merely appropriate blessing that fits the scheme; otherwise Sarah might not have endangered the entire scene. Her laughter, whether overheard or understood by the guests in another manner, threatens to undo the balance and exchange established between the three and Abraham. After all, the strangers reveal their identity, or at least the name of the power in whose name they speak, by replying to Sarah: "Is anything too wonderful for YHWH?" (v. 14). It may be that their promise is a threat to Abraham's role as host, upsetting it with the enormity of their blessing. This of course raises the question of whether Abraham knows the identity of his guests. Though he may have been able to discern that they could in fact be served as guests, he would likely not have asked their identity for fear of upsetting the balance of hospitality.[23] So it seems likely that he and Sarah did not know exactly whom they were hosting and that the only invocation of the name of God occurred in conjunction with Sarah's disbelief. Certainly their pledge to return does not insult Sarah. Abraham's very treatment of them — to meet them at the tree, to host them in such a way as to not delay them very long — indicates that the act of hospitality is only temporary (v. 3). Abraham does not seek to make the strangers permanent members of his and Sarah's community, to endure fully the transition from temporary-insider to member of the community.[24] The guests need to respond; they do, but they disturb their host's hospitality.

2.3. An Exchanged Gift without Obligation

In order to clarify what sort of gift this promise might be, we must briefly revisit the two major types of gift we have sketched. This could be a pure gift or it could be a gift purified of its possibility of violence while retaining reciprocity and exchange. Since we define a promise as an extended and doubled gift, both alternatives require consideration as we interpret the strangers' offer. Hospitality demands a counter-gift, yet the strangers appear to give only a pledge, either overwhelming the host with their promise and so snatching from Abraham the honor of being their host, or else failing entirely by giving a blessing that offends by its emptiness and impossibility. Engaging the pure

---

23. "Hosts could not ask questions which pried into the affairs of a guest although guests could volunteer information." Matthews and Benjamin, "The Host and the Stranger," p. 86.

24. Pitt-Rivers distinguishes between a hospitality that initiates guests into the community and one that does so only temporarily. Pitt-Rivers, "The Law of Hospitality," p. 111.

gift and its expectations will enable us to see how the promise can enter into the circle that Mauss described while remaining free from its obligations and potential conflicts. Thus, promise can be both a pure and an exchanged gift.

The first way to consider this offer would be to hold that the pledge of a son to the childless couple shocks because it, being nothing or perhaps beyond all being, escapes the obligations that Mauss discovered in the archaic gift. It cannot be fixed into the pattern of cause and effect, the ordinary field of action, and the world of substantial bodies. Derrida contends that it is necessary to look for such a gift because every merely ontic gift is one whose being is among other beings. Such a gift is ensconced within the force that beings exert on one another, the realm of metaphysics and ontotheology. This latter term loosely describes a way of thinking about beings that considers God, creatures, and everything else on the same plane and in the same sort of being, even if one differentiates God from all the rest in some way, perhaps through a distinction like the finite and infinite. God and being are tied together through same logos or rule. This, we may say, is the ontological correlate of Mauss's circle. Marion follows Derrida in part by describing the archaic gift as determined by cause and effect and so merely metaphysical:

> This system [of Mauss's potlatch] in fact remains thoroughly metaphysical: the giver gives the gift in the role of the efficient cause, mobilizing a formal and material cause (in order to define and reify the gift), and pursuing a final cause (the good of the givee and/or the glory of the giver).[25]

If this charge sticks to the exchanged gift, the obligations that weave people together are in fact a fruit of metaphysical causality since the gift causes the return gift. In their terminology, which relies on Martin Heidegger's description of ontotheology, they wish to describe causality in a metaphysical sense as an exacting system of cause, agent, and effect that wholly determine being. So we can see how a promise requires a post-metaphysical approach.

This might lead us to identify the promise as a pure gift. A further reason that the promise is so challenging to Sarah is that it contradicts her ordinary expectations. The strangers' blessing is so surprising that we might say that it is unwelcome. Thus, we could say that it is either too little or too much; the promise of a son does not merely answer or repeat the act of hospitality

---

25. Jean-Luc Marion, *Being Given: Toward a Phenomenology of Givenness*, trans. Jeffrey L. Kosky (Stanford: Stanford University Press, 2002), p. 75. Derrida makes a similar claim about an exchanged gift as an efficient cause: "In any case, if the gift or the event, if the event of the gift must remain unexplainable by a system of efficient causes, it is the effect of nothing; it is no longer an effect at all." *Given Time*, p. 123.

undertaken by Abraham. It poses a stranger alternative to a simple counter-gift since it is an incredible promise. Promises need to be believed in order for them to function well. To go beyond belief is to exceed expectation of what the gift asks for. The archaic gift seeks an equivalent; to fulfill it in a beneficial form of reciprocity, guests must repeat in a different way their host's offering, offering a gift that matches. To give more or less is to declare war or to shame the host.

But we can also consider the strangers' gift in terms of whether they give something, something that has being. An appropriate and expected counter-gift that matches Abraham's offer of hospitality has being, is graspable, and can be measured and compared to the original. In this scene, the strangers do not give anything: they give a promise, they give exactly nothing, and they give the impossible, since the patriarchal couple cannot bear children. To state that the gift is more or less than expected in this sense is to state, onto-logically, that it either is beyond being entirely or has no being whatsoever. We can take both positions as post-metaphysical (or even non-metaphysical) in character so far as they remove themselves from the realm of being or be-ings; we need not discuss whether such a hyper-essentialism is nihilistic.[26] This is the pure gift in many of its forms. In such a claim for the hyperbolic character of this kind of gift, it would never appear, would have no substance, could not be caused, and would never participate in the circle of exchange. If we were to define promise in this sense, it would therefore be an extra-ontological gift, perhaps shedding any contact with the realm of being at all.

To take promise as pure gift does have some advantages, particularly since it seems that it would prevent the gift from ever becoming an unwelcome offering, a poisoned gift that is secretly an act of domination. To avoid this kind of gift seems to be one of Derrida's primary motives.[27] While Mauss concedes the existence of the gift and leaves potlatches to be determined via more specific protocols in each culture, Derrida takes Mauss's analysis to have delineated what one might specify as the conditions of the impossibility of

---

26. It is important to recognize that nihilism is not merely an embrace of nothing as a kind of being. Other modalities are certainly possible. See Conor Cunningham, *Genealogy of Nihilism* (London: Routledge, 2000).

27. "It [the pure gift] offers us new resources of analysis, it alerts us to the traps of the would-be gift without debt, it activates our critical or ethical vigilance. It permits us always to say: 'Careful, you think there is a gift, dissymmetry, generosity, expenditure, or loss, but the cir-cle of debt, of exchange, or of symbolic equilibrium reconstitutes itself according to the laws of the unconscious; the 'generous' or 'grateful' consciousness is only the phenomenon of a calcula-tion and the ruse of an economy. Calculation and ruse, economy in truth would be the truth of these phenomena [these putatively free gifts]." Derrida, *Given Time*, pp. 15-16.

the gift. This impossibility is important for more than theoretical reasons because it makes us wary of any gift claiming to be free. Since Derrida expects a gift to be pure and carry no subterranean force to demand a counter-gift, Mauss's construal of an exchanged gift means the gift can never appear in freedom and always shows up with strings well attached.

A promise, if it were a pure gift, would betray the same interruptive or an-economic conditions, to use Derrida's language. He writes, "A gift could be possible, there could be a gift only at the instant an effraction in the circle will have taken place, at the instant all circulation will have been interrupted and on the condition of this instant."[28] This means that a promise would always draw attention to the failures of ordinary gifts, of gifts that demand reciprocity. This means that a promise that interrupts is critical; it calls attention to the lock-step causality of the archaic gift, of the limitations of the circle. This critical function of promise is worth preserving and developing since the laughter and the promise together provide a critical and irruptive moment in the narrative. Both short-circuit the back-and-forth of hospitality and both call attention to the impossibility of the child of promise and YHWH's promise to bring the impossible about. Both raise the question of whether this hospitality is a just or beneficial reciprocity or whether is it intimating domination, a relationship between host as master and guests as servants.

In applying the pure gift to the scene near Mamre, Derrida would seem to agree that the initial word offered by the strangers to Abraham and Sarah is at best nothing, at worst the gift changed into poison, an attempt to dupe or sidetrack the couple. Since a promise consists not of a single gift but a doubled and extended one, the initial token does not circumscribe the whole of the promise and therefore Derrida's determination of the impossibility of a pure gift seems to apply to the token, but not the whole of the promise. Further features, such as the doubling of the initial token and the trust required for a promise, will also show how Derrida's analysis applies only in part to a promise since the recipient's trust in the promise allows for an exchange to occur without obligation.

The two other characteristics of the pure gift are its oblique or interruptive relationship to the circular exchange of gifts in an ordinary sense and therefore its relationship to narrative. In the course of this analysis, Derrida shifts from considering the economy of gifts to what he called the economy of narrative. Rather than thinking through the causality of human practice, he takes up the flow of gifts within narrative, the interaction of event, character, and plot. These elements are shared by the phenomenon of promise as we

28. Derrida, *Given Time*, p. 9.

have it in the Hospitality of Abraham and Sarah owing to its doubled and extended character. While one might think that the pure gift has nothing to do with the circle of exchange, it is in fact the case that it does: "Now the gift, *if there is any,* would no doubt be related to economy. One cannot treat the gift, this goes without saying, without treating this relation to economy, even to the money economy. But is not the gift, if there is any, also that which interrupts economy?"[29] The relationship that the pure gift bears to the gift that is exchanged is that it interrupts or tears the economy or narrative it confronts:

> The event and the gift, the event as gift, the gift as event must be irruptive, unmotivated — for example, disinterested. They are decisive and they must therefore tear the fabric, interrupt the continuum of a narrative that nevertheless they call for, they must perturb the order of causalities.[30]

It does not circulate and so "it must not in any case be exhausted, as a gift, by the process of exchange."[31]

Thus the pure gift's existence depends upon the economy it interrupts. Unless one renders the promise entirely alien from the reciprocated gift, it must bear some kind of relationship. We may wonder, therefore, how pure the pure gift might be if it always is obliquely related to a particular economy, whether a local society or a particular narrative such as those Derrida considered. He noted that the pure gift's interruptive relationship to the narrative of Baudelaire's "Counterfeit Money" is that it interrupts the narrative in a surprising manner.[32] The unexpected character of the promise is its ability to exceed the expectations of Abraham and Sarah for the proper behavior of their guests. They are obligated to give, but they give *nothing* and they give *more*. Their promise is not readily available; it could be thwarted or empty. They need not promise and so they are free from the obligation to give. Nothing in the hospitality offered provokes them to this excessive promise, other than the occasion to bless their host. They give more without giving anything.

Likewise, if the promise were not doubled into an initial pledge and a final gift, Sarah's rejection would signal a refused gift. Marion, like Derrida, has taken the refused gift as the primary way to find the pure gift.[33] Refusal, in other words, does not stop the donation if the gift is pure; the archaic gift is

---

29. Derrida, *Given Time,* p. 7.

30. Derrida, *Given Time,* p. 123.

31. Derrida, *Given Time,* p. 7.

32. This is how he seems to rely on the role of the pure gift in narrative since it cannot appear and cannot have antecedents nor be brought about as an effect tendered by a cause.

33. Marion, *Being Given,* pp. 74-78.

stopped, its cycles frozen, if one of the agents fails to reciprocate or accept the gift given. It might seem that Sarah's laughter, if it were only a refusal and rejection of the visitors' blessing, would indicate that the promise is a pure gift. The guests, clearly upset by Sarah's laughter as indicated in their questions (vv. 13, 15), nevertheless still hold true to their offer of a promise. All rests in their statement of the possibility that abides in YHWH (v. 14). So the doubled character of the gift can bear its refusal and indicate that the promise need not be accepted by its recipient. In spite of the lack of credibility the strangers may have had in Sarah's eyes, they will still, in the name of YHWH, hold to their pledge.

The agency of a promise requires closer attention, since it seems to respond to a particular demand, that is, to bless the host, yet is free of it. Marion has developed another way of confronting the gift that considers this causality. He follows Derrida in claiming that Mauss's description provides the conditions for the impossibility of the gift. But he is not coy about the gift in the same way as Derrida, seeking it out by utilizing a phenomenological *epoche* to bracket out the various dimensions of the gift in order for it to appear in and of itself. This, in drastic summary, requires Marion to bracket in turn the giver, the recipient, and finally the gift itself. He discovers, at the end of his analysis, nothing but pure givenness, a gift that is outside being.[34]

Since nothing can remove the gift from this chain of causality in the world of being, Marion aims to remove the gift from the realm of being for another reason than just that of force and domination. He claims that the phenomenological reduction to givenness can discover the gift outside of or otherwise than being, in other words, a non-metaphysical concept. But we do not need to consider the full conclusion of his reduction to givenness since we can show how promise is outside of and within the causes. The act of promising is free; it does not cause trust, and can be distrusted without the consequences that attend a rejected gift. All these indicate that the causality of the promise is not bound by the kind of ontotheology Marion has criticized. Promise is neither metaphysical in the negative sense that Heidegger and his followers criticize nor is it utterly non-metaphysical in Marion's sense.

One need not follow Marion and Derrida to exceed being in order to find the promise offered at Mamre as gift; one could attempt to account for the promise by taking up another aspect of the logic of gift exchange with Pierre Bourdieu and John Milbank. For them, I do not discharge my debt by immediately returning a gift to you; rather, gift exchange requires time, and,

---

34. Marion, *Being Given*, p. 80.

as Bourdieu writes, non-identical repetition.[35] The counter-gift must bear some similarity to the initial gift. This is why in the situation of hospitality one usually thinks a true counter-gift to be the reversal of roles, with the former host becoming a guest to the one she or he had hosted. One would not consider this counter-gift to be identical to the first but it repeats the first in that it offers the same significance. It does not threaten an escalation of giving, as Mauss notes can occur in Melanesia, when a subsequent recipient shows his or her superiority by offering more.[36] By repeating the previous gift, the competition of giving in the form of giving more or less is purged. We may call this the purified gift. It has much to offer our consideration of promise since it upholds exchange without force. Also, this gift does not exhaustively describe the character of promise as a gift.

Milbank has made use of this definition of a purified gift, a gift that is in some sense the fulfillment of the archaic gift without the purity of the vector in order to reform Marion's and Derrida's conception of the gift. Of his many critical remarks on their proposals, Milbank most interestingly objects to the unilateralist view of the gift that they uphold. Milbank retains the reciprocal constitution of the gift but fits it to other schemata than the agonistic giving and metaphysical chains of causality that Marion identifies; he is chastened by the problems engendered by inserting a gift within the immanent field of give-and-take, the field of metaphysics. Instead, he suspends the gift within the repetition of the divine life itself. "And if the created interplay between Being and beings . . . participates in the constitutive distance between Father and Son, then we, as creatures, only *are* as sharing in God's arrival, his forgiving, and perpetual eucharist."[37] Thus, he seeks not a pure gift that lacks any return but, he notes, a sort of purified gift that avoids the agonism and competitive nature of the gift while upholding the reciprocity involved in it. Mauss documents many instances where the gift circle becomes increasingly violent as more and more is given. This and several other elements of the potlatch must be purged while recognizing the reciprocity that makes the gift in an archaic sense.[38] For instance, it seems that there can be no neutral territory

35. Pierre Bourdieu, *Outline of a Theory of Practice*, trans. Richard Nice (Cambridge: Cambridge University Press, 1977), pp. 3-5.

36. Mauss, *The Gift*, p. 37.

37. Milbank, "Can a Gift Be Given?" p. 154.

38. This is also the approach that Paul Ricoeur takes in *Amour et justice* (Paris: Seuil, 2008), pp. 13-42. Ricoeur distinguishes between the gift that is superabundant (our pure gift) yet related to the ordinary gift of equivalence (our archaic gift); he holds that both kinds of gift need one another to have practical and theoretical significance. See John Wall, *Moral Creativity: Paul Ricoeur and the Poetics of Possibility* (Oxford: Oxford University Press, 2005).

or sphere that lies between God and creation as there are between peoples. To do so, in Milbank's view, would be to admit that there is reality or being that is not from God or to conclude that God could receive and gain from a gift returned to God. Both violate God as the sole source of all being, in Milbank's view: "Counter-gift cannot possibly be predicated of God, since there is nothing extra to God that could return to him. God gives 'to' no-one, but creates all ex nihilo, causes all by his grace and goes on giving despite all refusals."[39] So, God's gifts, according to Milbank, do not linger without effect.[40] Since a promise is extended it can linger where those promised may freely refuse or accept the token.

On Milbank's view, one might take a promise to merely indicate the moment between the repetitions of the initial gift. But doubling is not repetition; the idea of the repetition of gifts is a way to continue a single gift and its return through another counter-gift. A promise consists of a doubled gift; in no sense can the doubling be one gift and then another that is returned in relationship to the first. The promise is the extended gift of a donor; it admits exchange within it but its two poles, the pledge of Isaac and Isaac himself, are the sole gift of YHWH. The doubling belongs to one continuous flow of giving, the promise's extension. Similarly, because Milbank does not express the irruptive and oblique character of the gift that marks the pure gift, he has to develop other resources for thinking of God's gift as a critical and creative act.

The extension of the promise opens up space within it for free exchange. As in Milbank's proposal, the promise does not merely interrupt the life of Sarah and Abraham. It does not merely give them pause. It offers a way to fulfill their expectation of a child beyond all hope. It allows the utterly impossible to appear which turns out to be the deeply longed-for desire. This impossibility and desire Gillian Allnutt puts rightly in her poem: "It's hidden, the hurt, like a hard little bird in the tent/of her heart. She's tended it."[41] Sarah rejects and welcomes the promise at the same time. The recipient of a promise, when trusting, anticipates the future gift and so can count on its arrival. We can see this negatively in Sarah's laughter. She rejects the pledge because this blessing is empty — it is incredible and unexpected. She treats this offer as nothing; she can doubt it, particularly since it does not fit; it does not cohere with what she takes to be possible. This amounts to nearly a rejection of the counter-gift. Even if the gift of a son did involve delay, the strangers offer

39. Milbank, "Can a Gift Be Given?" p. 134.

40. "The divine gift never . . . hovers in a desert. If it did, then it would indeed reside in a space 'outside' Being, indifferent to it." Milbank, "Can a Gift Be Given?" p. 137.

41. Gillian Allnutt, "Sarah's Laughter," in How the Bicycle Shone: New & Selected Poems (Tarset: Bloodaxe Books, 2007), p. 99.

something initially. Thus she cannot take their pledge, lacking this trust, as a suitable conclusion to the delicate encounter that occurs at Mamre.

Sarah's laugher shows how a promise interacts with an ordinary reciprocated gift, fulfilling the demand of the gift economy's drift toward equivalence. The token appears as a gift so far as the recipient trusts. This requires pause since the trust offered is not wholly generated out of the subject that the promise confronts. Yet, one can imagine that the same pledge offers for some a gift that anticipates the final offering of a son and for others nothing at all. The strangers' pledge meets incredulity, finding it out while Sarah listens from within the tent. So, if a recipient trusts, one can then take this as a gift even though it is not yet the final gift and offer in return a counter-gift to God or to others. Trust allows Sarah and Abraham to take this nothing or something, this indeterminate blessing from the strangers, as a proper counter-gift to theirs though it is not sure, though it surprises. Since this offer has neither force nor need to be accepted, it is an exchange within the ordinary economy of hospitality while giving freedom to its recipients. We can imagine a scenario where Sarah and Abraham rejoice and accept this promise and take no offense at this striking conclusion to the scene of hospitality.

So, we can see that neither the pure nor the purified gift will do to fully account for the promise as gift. Both notions of gift we have examined here preserve the logic of reciprocity in Mauss's analysis, albeit purified of its archaic potential for escalation or bad reciprocity, or they present a form of the gift that lacks all exchange by the utter impossibility of the gift's arrival as pure gift. Promise, as a gift, properly lies between the two forms of a pure and purified gift. It upholds the nature of exchange within the field of love created by the initial token but defers the obligation that any gift bears. It interrupts the economy of exchange by the strange being of the promised token. Since it bears the functions of both, one need not resort to the extra-ontological (and extra-ontic) gift of Marion but one can take advantage of Derrida's attention to how the gift irrupts Mauss's potlatch and gives time. Yet it does not lack the unilateral dimension of the pure gift, an offering that demands no return. The promise is offered entirely on its own since it is first given and then extended until the promise is delivered. Thus, when taken from either the perspective of the archaic or the pure gift, a promise seems to be nothing at all or beyond being altogether. Promise, rather, skirts between the two as a perhaps, and as a possibility. It engages Mauss's potlatch while carving out its own space through doubling and extending the initial pledge given to its fulfillment.

This requires more attention to the being of the gift offered in promise to further identify the specific difference of promise from these gifts. Take yet again the phenomena present in Sarah and Abraham's hospitality: they are offered nothing but a pledge after welcoming the three strangers. Sarah is incredulous and rejects this pledge with her doubt and laughter. In an ancient setting of hospitality, hosts welcomed strangers in order to domesticate them; strangers could turn against hosts as their enemy. Sarah's laughter endangers this delicate scene, her life, and the honor of all the parties involved. The strangers could take this laughter as a rejection of their pledge and acceptance of themselves as enemies, not friends. Sarah attempts to hide the laughter and the strangers point out they heard it, marking her rejection. Yet they persist and further bind the name of this child to this rejection and laughter. Isaac's very name reflects the contested nature of the pledge. As the double of the promise offered by the strangers, Isaac bears Sarah's rejection in his name, "He laughs." Isaac himself seems to be an extended gift that always refers to this scene of hospitality, to the incredible promise, and to Sarah's laughter.

2.4. Opening

If promising involves a risk, this deserves closer consideration since it would imply that God becomes party to doubling and extension, perhaps even involving doubling and extension in God's own being. This dimension of the phenomenon of promise means that promise has its being as possibility and that it does not merely give being and time but gives them as possibility and as a transformation and critique of what is given, whether it is creation, institutions, persons, or time itself.

We can discover the priority of the possible if we consider the exchange that occurs between the donor and the recipient of the promise. The indeterminate nature of the pledge that gives rise to Sarah's laughter bespeaks this possibility. Trust in the promise anticipates its fulfillment; this trust gives honor or glory to God. If the divine name is given in conjunction with the pledged token, it may seem that both trust and God's accomplishment of the promise constitute the name itself. It may further seem that trust has a hand in giving God God's name just as God would stake God's name in the act of promising, risking God's reputation, as it were. Yet in this doxology it grants or suspends the token as if it were the final gift itself. This "as if" matters since it sustains the being of the promise as possibility. Should the "if" translate into either nothing or actuality, the promise is lost since it would collapse its extension and reduce its doubling to a reciprocated gift, a pure one, or nothing at all. If it were to translate into nothing, the promise would be just wishful thinking or the impossible. If it assumed being, the pledge would become the whole of the promise and nothing further would be expected. A promise would then be an ordinary reciprocated gift.

This is why the character of a promise and its final gift must be held out as possibility and distance, distance in the sense of continued and extended giving. One might fear that the final gift then would collapse the promise and it would afterwards be considered a final gift and therefore bear with it the obligation that any ordinary gift would bring. The extension of a promise shows that even though the final gift may be given, it never ceases to be given, an insight we may draw from Milbank's proposal. The giving of the promise may be fulfilled but it never terminates and so would reify the arrival of the fulfillment into a gift that would bear with it a demand. This dimension of the phenomenon of promise will gain more substance when we consider Pentecost and the promise of the Spirit in the next chapter.

To reiterate: promising is a specific kind of gift, a doubled and extended gift. The patriarchal couple receives from the strangers a dubious counter-gift; they expect one yet the pledge of a son causes conflict between the strangers and, at least, Sarah. Such a token as their pledge has a middle existence between the concrete gift and no gift at all. It could be a gift or it could be folly. So, at first, a promise has an initial gift that lies between existence and non-existence. The kind of existence — neither being nor nothing — but rather possibility or a kind of wonder characterizes the promise. It does not appear nor is it entirely impossible. A promise may interrupt the ordinary economy of gift; it does not wrench the circle of exchange entirely out of its shape. Rather, it enters into the various gifts and counter-gifts between the various webs of human relations, national action, and familial intercourse. The promise offers first a token that interrupts one circle to open up another. It is disjointed with Sarah's expectation but manages to establish a new plot nonetheless: one that is surprising yet does not eclipse the hospitality of Sarah and Abraham. As the strangers state, nothing is too wonderful for YHWH.

As we have noted, the pledge the guests offer is not a gift on its own and therefore requires no counter-gift. Abraham and Sarah are not indebted to the strangers by their promise of a son's birth; indeed, the superficial character of a promise means that when dealing with an initial pledge one could be dealing equally with wishes or pathology just as much as with a trustworthy note. Sarah, in this sense of the promise, is right to reject it.

We may now draw together the elements of promise. It consists of four matters: the initial gift, the trust or distrust of the one promised, the field created by that trust and the extension of the gift between the pledge and its fulfillment, and the fulfillment itself. Subsequent to the promise lies the action and power of God, a weak power that distinguishes it from other forms of promising that we must consider, kinds of promising that degrade the graciousness of God and the true power of the Crucified One. Each dimension of the phenomena of promise demonstrates important theological opportunities for investigation. We are hardly finished with the gift. It demands and gives time as much as it creates an opening for a genuine human return, a gift to others. This we call nothing less than Eucharist, the place of promise.

CHAPTER 3

Weakness and Time

What we will be has not yet been revealed.

1 John 3:2

Promise is a gift of time that liberates its recipients. It is a gift offering time where time has run out. As a doubled and extended gift, God's promise does not merely stretch out one's time to anticipate the future in longing expectation, but it also creates time by opening a field of love, and introducing time that was not looked for, that was beyond all hope. The time of God's promise is not limited to the delivery of the promise, since the gift God gives is God's own Spirit; the arrival of that which is promised does not nullify the promise. There is no afterwards to the promise, no time in which the promise is past. Pentecost is a feast where there is no *post festum.* God's promise has no closure or completion.

This creative and critical act of promise permits the emergence of new time by granting possibility and therefore agency to those who trust the promise. Promise thus unites the expected and unexpected. Pentecost, God's outpouring of the Spirit, is this event of promise and our way into the consideration of time and gift. The Spirit has classically been described as God's very gift, both by Augustine and Basil of Caesarea.[1] By examining how the descent of the Spirit, a gift given without measure, opens the future, we will see how Pentecost exercises a weak power and brings forth the possibility given in God's outpouring of the Spirit on the bodies of creation and of Christ.

This summary of the relationship between time and promise requires

1. Basil, *Du Spiritu Sancti* 25; Augustine, *De Trinitate* 15.5.

explication, emerging from further analysis of promise and gift from the perspective of temporality, the extension and doubling of the gift in the promise in time. God's promise gives time by transforming given time, the time one already has. If ordinary time is cyclical, characterized by the return of the same, the promise does not wholly negate that circle; it does not remove the ordinary out of its locale, but transforms it, criticizes it, and offers it new existence.

The promise further gives time by allowing for action, opening up the freedom that is the future as it grants possibility. And most of all, it does not delay the giving of a gift as a strategy or means of domination. The practice of promise can be distinguished, as can reciprocity, into beneficial and injurious promises. In promising, God gives Godself over as one promising in order to free the past. But there are other ways that promise could operate, ways that a promise could create an obligation despite our efforts to show otherwise in the previous chapter. The extension of a promise, the necessary delay between the initial offering of promise and its fulfillment, could be a way to dominate the other through the delay of giving by leading on the trusting recipient of the promise. Thus, Hannah Arendt praises promise, while Friedrich Nietzsche censures it. Arendt sees its power as extending the present into the future, or at least mastering and extending the present into the future, despite what may challenge, alter, or undermine the present state of affairs. Nietzsche also allows for the future tense of promise, but has more interest in interdicting it for the way that promise requires the domination of the past over the present. He claims that the promise, since it is anchored in the past, does not afford the emergence of the truly new and strange. Likewise, he holds that it allows the past to be a negative and painful force on the present.

Beyond this sense that Arendt and Nietzsche offer as promise as power over time, the time of the promise is a gracious time, a time that does not carry with it the poison of the past, the terror of the future, or the prison of the present. But it also does not abandon those tenses of time, negating them utterly or asking one to utterly squelch the past from memory. It seeks to liberate those times as well as to grant new time. It meets those kinds of time and it transforms them, criticizes them, and opens them up as new time. This gracious creation of and interaction with ordinary time shows why promise fits God's giving better than many of the unilateralist models of gift that theologians advocate. A gift that never welcomes or obtains a return, one that denies reciprocity, must always reconfigure expectation into the world of the present rather than temporally past or future.

This important action of promise to give time requires us to consider in what way or how the promise has such power. It could exercise itself to offer a gift unilaterally or in an effort of dominance. Instead of these negative instances of power, we shall see that the phenomenon of Pentecost, the out-pouring of the Spirit, occurs in what Walter Benjamin calls a weak power, or, to use musical language, the Spirit who works in *pianissimo*.

Any consideration of the gift needs to take up the question of time, even if one must ultimately claim in the course of one's analysis that time is utterly uninvolved with and exterior to the gift. Time in this chapter refers to the passage of time that obtains following the offering of a gift. Time holds a place of importance in a construal of the gift when reciprocity or exchange figures into the definition of the gift. When one advances a unilateral view of the gift, one that does not consider exchange or reciprocity as an essential part of gift-giving, then time does not matter since there is no delay between the offering of a gift, unless, as in Derrida's case, one considers the gift itself to be the gift of time.[2] The event of the gift in this case can be considered in analog to the lightning strike from above, the *Sendkrecht von Oben*. One may hold that the unilateral gift can obtain a response that is not a counter-gift in any proper sense and so hold that what happens after the gift is exterior to it, but that would obfuscate the archaic gift's circular path while claiming to articulate a pure and unilateral gift. To hold, instead, that the gift obtains a counter-gift or that it is itself an extended and doubled gift as in our analysis of promise is to show that time is not only intrinsic to the gift but also given by it.

This unilateralist position can seem very attractive to theologians who articulate God's grace as fundamentally other than the world or who resist attributing agency to God on account of God's eternity, perhaps taking as their point of departure something like Karl Barth's famous description of grace encountering the world as a tangent to a circle.[3]

However, such a hyperbolic approach to the gift sidesteps a crucial hermeneutical and theological problem. In interpretive terms, the gift that has no relationship to reciprocity or what is already given cannot interact with what comes before the gift, the field into which the gift is given, in any other way than to erase it, to trump it, to completely overcome and end that economy. The pure gift does not allow us any interpretive approach to the given except negation, erasure, and interruption. We may signal this problem in theological terms by invoking the tumultuous relationship between grace

---

2. John Milbank claims that the gift of time in Derrida is a gift of "the passing away of time." See Milbank, "Can a Gift Be Given? Prolegomena to a Future Trinitarian Metaphysic," *Modern Theology* 11 (1995): 131. Rather, as interruption, the gift of time in Derrida is the flash in the circuit of ordinary, circular time.

3. "In the resurrection the new world of the Holy Spirit touches the old world of the flesh. But it touches it as a tangent to a circle, which is, without touching it." Karl Barth, *Der Römerbrief, Zweite Fassung 1922* (Zürich: Theologischer Verlag, 1989), p. 6.

and nature, or grace and creation. Now, creation cannot be equated with that which we take as the given, since God's good creation can be distorted and subjected. If God's gift is oblique to the economy of creation and does not address the given in any way, that gift leaves the rest of creation in a lurch since the ordinary run of the world takes time and rests on what is given, what is first offered in God's continued act of preservation of creation. The gift that does not interact critically to transform that which is given in creation, the field of existence, leaves the "unassumed the unhealed." By contrast, the archaic gift only and always directly responds to the already existing field of the given but it could never offer anything new or transcend it.[4] In attending to the phenomenon of Pentecost, we shall see that the gift of the Spirit, the descent of the Spirit to rest upon the body of the church, is a gracious promise, a weak power, and a gift of time.[5]

We mean time here as time construed as the faculty of change or the agency of creatures. Time, as a natural and human element, can be considered in many different kinds of analysis. Empirical studies in the social and natural sciences privilege a form of time that can be repeated and measured, so-called "clock time." The tradition of analytical philosophy has developed a rigorous discourse of time that extends far beyond a division of two camps adhering to either an "A" or "B" series of time.[6] Psychological and psychoanalytical studies bridge the gaps between empirical and literary study. The French anthropological tradition and phenomenology both offer additional resources for considering time.[7] While the first kinds of time may add dimensions of analysis to the consideration of promise that the ones I privilege lack, phenomenology explicitly makes available a form of time that bears on human practice in addition to enabling theology to discuss ontology and being after the scuttled and sunk project of metaphysics has passed to the depths. This will fur-

4. Paul Ricoeur shows how there is an important way that the archaic gift in its poisonous or dangerous form can be transformed for the better through sacrifice in *Parcours de la reconnaissance: Trois études* (Paris: Gallimard, 2001), pp. 374-77. Rowan Williams offers this as a way to reinterpret Jesus' refusal of violence and his acceptance of torture, scourging, and crucifixion as the way to end the exchange of blows that constitutes the economy of gift as violence. *Resurrection: Interpreting the Easter Gospel*, rev. ed. (Cleveland: Pilgrim Press, 2002), pp. 5-13.

5. A full evaluation of this form of giving with respect to others and its suitability for theological doctrines of grace lies outside of this project.

6. The analytical and anthropological traditions are summed up well in Alfred Gell, *The Anthropology of Time: Cultural Constructions of Temporal Maps and Images* (Providence: Berg, 1992).

7. A useful discussion of time in the phenomenological tradition is David Couzens Hoy, *The Time of Our Lives: A Critical History of Temporality* (Cambridge: MIT Press, 2009).

ther allow us to consider time and place as dimensions of God's promise in ways that are not dominated by space. The metaphysical construction of being as presence is primarily as a spatial presence and so a subordination of time to space, the spatialization of modernity.[8] Considering the nature of time and power will allow us to discuss the post-metaphysical concept of possibility that it requires and offers, post-metaphysical here meaning possibility freed from its dependence on actuality. This will bear, then, both on the sort of human agency that follows and on the love that can well up in the middle of promise in the impure gift in the next chapter, concluding in the final chapter with a survey of the Eucharist as the place of promise.

Therefore, we will first consider power and then possibility. By taking up anthropological explanations of why people give and exchange gifts we will revisit the question of the force or obligation that gifts bear from the perspective of the time gift-exchange demands. This will enable us to situate Arendt's enthusiasm for a strong form of promise and Nietzsche's ambivalence toward promise within a consideration of power and gift and show the weak force of Pentecost. Discussion of this power will allow us to outline the kind of possibility given by the promise. This will show that the possibility that promise offers is that being between something and nothing that we uncovered when considering the Hospitality of Abraham and Sarah. This possibility is directed toward the other.

3.1. Pentecost

The icon of Pentecost in the Eastern Orthodox traditions depicts the orientation to possibility and the future that biblical writing about the Spirit affords. The icon, also known as The Descent of the Holy Spirit, consists of the descent of the Spirit on a group of disciples, which includes more than just the Twelve at the time of Pentecost as depicted in Acts 2. Sometimes the group includes the evangelists and Paul. These figures represent not only specific disciples or apostles but also all those on whom the Spirit descended prior to Pentecost; some figures conflate the apostolic community and saints from the Old Testament.

Sometimes the icon has a gap in it. The space at the head of the group is often left open while other times the Virgin Mary sits at the head of the group.[9] Jesus is both absent and present in the icon; since the descent of the

---

8. This is the subject of Chapter 5, "The Topology of Promise," below.

9. Some commentators, like Ouspensky, hold that the icon is orderly to represent the

Spirit occurs after his ascension to the right hand of the Father, Jesus cannot appear as such in the picture and so the head of the assembly should represent that absence. His body, however, occurs as the assembly, the body of Christ. Jesus is present, abiding in the assembly as they abide in him. The descent of the Spirit binds this community to Jesus and his way of the cross to embrace what may come.

But we do not just have an icon that gives a window to the future since at the base of the assembled recipients of the Spirit sits either a multitude of people or an aged royal figure. Leonid Ouspensky captures this symbolic tradition, in which this king stands in for all people waiting for liberation. He writes, "In ancient manuscripts, the multitude, mentioned in the Acts of the Apostles, is represented at the bottom of the composition. Yet very soon it was replaced by one symbolical figure of a king, personifying the people or peoples, with the inscription 'Cosmos.'"[10] The gift of the Spirit is a gift for the future that concerns the past as well as the present, embracing all of time. Pentecost does not simply come from the future full-stop; it dwells intimately in the past. No pure amnesia enters in with the Spirit's embrace, no erasure of what once was; the old is made new, not swept away. Stressing the future at the expense of the past would require such forgetfulness.

In its broadest strokes, this icon depicts the narrative of Pentecost in Acts 2. This text has been read as a kind of culmination of the Tower of Babel, a fulfillment of the prophet Joel, and an altogether new event, even though some lines of scholarship hold that Luke never understood the Spirit to operate after Jesus' absence in any way differently than before.[11] Happily, this icon obscures any such before-and-after since it discloses the descent of the Spirit onto all of creation together with the church. Pentecost is both new and old. Yet it does not simply repeat the work of the Spirit in creation, brooding. Instead, it represents the complexity of God's self-giving. God gives the Spirit yet here the Spirit descends after Jesus pleads for the Spirit's brooding. The Spirit's own work is to give himself again and more fully but his giving of himself is to empower the apostolic community to remain in Jesus, to share and be Jesus' cross-marked body, and to fulfill the longings of

---

tranquil hierarchy in the church. See Leonid Ouspensky and Vladimir Lossky, *The Meaning of Icons,* trans. G. E. H. Palmer and E. Kadloubovsky (Crestwood, NY: St. Vladimir's Seminary Press, 1982), p. 207. Mary disturbs this order when she is present, offering a tranquility that upsets only the hierarchy, not the order of the body.

10. Ouspensky and Lossky, *The Meaning of Icons,* p. 208.

11. Jacob Jervall, "Sons of the Prophets: The Holy Spirit in the Acts of the Apostles," in *The Unknown Paul: Essays on Luke-Acts and Early Christian History* (Minneapolis: Augsburg, 1984), pp. 96-121.

the nations and the groaning of all creation. Pentecost therefore allows for a discussion of the economy of creation and its renewal and transformation in the descent of the Spirit.

Though the icon of Pentecost privileges the depiction of events in Luke-Acts, its most important aim is to display that in this remarkable event the Spirit personally rests on the people of God and does not just distribute spiritual charisms that are alienated from the Spirit. This corresponds to Jesus' important discourse in John 3:23: that the Spirit is to be given without measure, descending in excess and not doled out in circumscribed lumps. In this strange discourse between Nicodemus and Jesus surrounding water, birth, and a second birth in the Spirit, Jesus claims that the Spirit is a measureless gift. The Spirit is given by Jesus and the Father as a doubled and extended gift. So does one have the Spirit in the event of Pentecost, in the prayer for the Spirit in baptism, or in the laying on of hands, or do we await the Spirit's full advent? Theologians have sometimes held that this shows that the Spirit offers gifts distinguished from the Spirit's very self.[12] But to call the Spirit a measureless gift is to show that the gift is always itself the Spirit and awaiting more of the same. As Basil of Caesarea writes, "the enlightenment the Spirit gives is himself."[13] This doubling and extension of the Spirit will allow us to see how this promise finally is not a ploy of delay but the ever-widening power of hope. It is, as Paul calls the Spirit, the *arrabon*, the down payment or pledge of the Reign of God (2 Cor. 5:5). Even the fulfillment of the promise does not mark its end or undoing. Hope continues since the Spirit is a measureless gift. I will show in the discussion that follows that this resting, dwelling, and descending upon what God has already given is the Spirit's gift of time. Pentecost is the event of the Triune God's promise.

3.2. Power and Promise

So that we can consider the power of Pentecost and its promise, we need to consider the interrelationship of time, gift, and power. Power and time has emerged among anthropologists in their analysis of gift as a crucial way to account for gift-giving practices and the nature of the obligations that the archaic gift possesses. We will connect power and time through Pierre Bour-

---

12. This has become in the West known as "created grace." For a summary, see Karl Rahner, "Some Implications of the Scholastic Concept of Uncreated Grace," in *Theological Investigations*, vol. 1, trans. Cornelius Ernst (New York: Seabury Press, 1961), pp. 319-46.

13. Basil, *Du Spiritu Sancti* 9.22.

dieu's work on gift-giving. Bourdieu considers gift-exchange as a way people exercise power over each other. Like most discussions of the gift in anthropology, this story begins with Marcel Mauss. According to Mauss, the exchange of gifts requires time.[14] Time does more than punctuate the interval between when one party meets its obligations or passes over them. The gift itself demands, creates, and offers time. The march of time does not merely measure events indifferently. This accords generally with Mauss's approach to give an account of gift-exchange from the perspective of his informants, the first-person explanations of gift-exchange. Thus, Mauss explains the gift as having an agency of its own following one informant's attribution of power to the gift in the guise of something he calls *hau*.[15] Mauss then strips this power of its mythical guise in his general attribution that things have agency when treated as a gift. This agency accounts for the time that obtains between the reception of a gift and the offering of another one in turn. Thus, Mauss famously describes the strange distortions of perception that a modern person discerns: things become people and people become things.[16] The *hau* will compel the gift to leave even if it takes on another form in another object and so the human agents end up being passive in exchange. The agency in the gift itself will drive time forward so that the term will be complete. If the recipient of the gift holds on to the gift, hoarding or squandering it, the gift will become poison once the term has eclipsed. Thus in Mauss's formulation, time is internal to the gift, not imposed on it from the perspective of an outsider or the external and neutral clock.

Claude Lévi-Strauss censures Mauss for this approach and considers him to have lost objectivity. In his attack on Mauss in his introduction to a volume of Mauss's work, time as a function of the exchange of gifts falls to a model of interpretation that purges time from its picture of the practice of gift-exchange.[17] To be sure, Lévi-Strauss acknowledges that one can only give and give again after a delay, but this is immaterial, for the law of reciprocity governs the exchange.[18] He considers this to be the proper scientific and objective formulation of why gifts are exchanged and the proper reciprocal

---

14. Marcel Mauss, *The Gift: The Form and Reason for Exchange in Archaic Society*, trans. W. D. Halls (New York: Norton, 1990), p. 35.

15. Mauss, *The Gift*, p. 11.

16. Mauss, *The Gift*, p. 14.

17. Claude Lévi-Strauss, "Introduction à l'oeuvre de Marcel Mauss," in Marcel Mauss, *Sociologie et Anthropologie*, ed. Georges Gurvitch (Paris: Presses Universitaires de France, 1950), p. xxxix.

18. Lévi-Strauss, "Introduction à l'oeuvre de Marcel Mauss," p. xlvi.

model of this practice. Lévi-Strauss purges time from the gift and replaces it with an iron law of circulation.

Bourdieu opposes this formulation in his *Outline of a Theory of Practice.*[19] Bourdieu expands Mauss's observation and gives it a critical tinge by construing exchange as governed by the power agents seek to gain over each other. For Bourdieu, gift-exchange is a fragile and tentative process that agents enact through their veiled attempts to dominate one another. Thus, anthropologists should not idealize gift-exchange in terms that privilege the gift apart from the perspective of the outsider and insider.

The strategy employed by agents makes gift-exchange work in Bourdieu's model. One party gives, one receives, and then later the receiving party offers a counter-gift either back to the first group or on to a third party. Bourdieu writes that such description of gift-exchange fails to observe the problems that can follow the offering or reception of a gift, problems introduced by the time that obtains between the offering of gifts and counter-gifts.[20] One can fail to reciprocate or try to show up others by giving even more in return, thus bringing the social relationships between the parties to either conflict or challenge. These observations do not advance beyond those catalogued by Mauss but Bourdieu tries to point out that they are all exercises of power over others, attempts to dominate and control the other party through the bait of honor and the avoidance of shame.

Bourdieu argues that people and groups use time strategically as a medium of force over others in the offering of gifts and to show that gifts themselves are the embodied force of that time.[21] Time does not pass indifferently before and after the gift is given. Once the gift appears, claims Bourdieu, the gift itself demands time, an appropriate length of time to occur before it demands the return of the gift, the fulfillment of obligations. Thus, we can note that Bourdieu sees that the gift-givers use time and can fall subject to time. The advent of a gift and the demand for a counter-gift constrains their actions just as much as it sets in motion the possibility of reciprocating the gift. So, Bourdieu provides the task at hand: to elaborate how the divine promise of the Spirit does not exert force in this way by demanding time or constricting agency in the ways he has outlined. In both considerations of the role of time in gift-giving, Bourdieu claims that the interrelationship between time and the gift is one of power or force. In order to show how Bourdieu's attribu-

19. Pierre Bourdieu, *Outline of a Theory of Practice,* trans. Richard Nice (Cambridge: Cambridge University Press, 1977).

20. Bourdieu, *Outline,* pp. 5-6.

21. Bourdieu, *Outline,* pp. 6-7.

tion of power to the gift does not apply to promise, we will take up and demonstrate how the act of promising that occurs in Pentecost is a weak power with reference to its openness to the future and its recovery of the past.

But let us first consider the case for taking promise as an instance of strong power by considering Arendt's and Nietzsche's examinations of promise. Each will expose the need to articulate how Pentecost is a weak power. Arendt discusses promise as a crucial dimension of political action in *The Human Condition*.[22] In her understanding, promise sustains political life by remedying two weaknesses that plague political life. These two problems are both forms of uncertainty. She writes that though political action is reasonable and deliberate, it suffers from the wavering human heart and the unintended consequences or outcomes of acts. Human beings may not hold the same commitments tomorrow that they do today; they may waver in their resolve on a course of action. This is the "darkness of the human heart."[23] Likewise, what people actually do suffers from an immense gap between decision and action. The results of any deeds may outstrip intention and resolve. Both of these problems confront the political and threaten it from within, from the actors themselves, or from without, since what follows from actions may exceed the purpose and role that the actions were intended to have.

Arendt holds that human promising remedies these two problems by exercising a control of the future, defending the present against these two kinds of contingencies. Promising binds the human being today in spite of future desires that may lead humans away from their commitments, because it is the "power of stabilization inherent in the faculty of making promises."[24] Likewise, when Arendt shows how promise can defend against the future, she shows how her view of promise is an effort that extends the present, the now, into the future, defending it against the unknown, the strange, and what may appear. "This superiority [of a people bound by promise] derives from the capacity to dispose of the future as though it were the present, that is, the enormous and truly miraculous enlargement of the very dimension in which power can be effective."[25] This view of promise sees it as a strong event, a strong power as opposed to our sense of a weak one in which promising is fragile and does not defend the present against the future but embraces it, makes way for it, and is willing to criticize what is given, is now for the sake of what may come. Arendt's view of promise constricts possibility and the kind

22. Hannah Arendt, *The Human Condition* (Chicago: University of Chicago Press, 1989).
23. Arendt, *The Human Condition*, p. 244.
24. Arendt, *The Human Condition*, p. 243.
25. Arendt, *The Human Condition*, p. 245.

of promise she advocates fits Bourdieu's sense of a practice that is an effort of power over the future.[26] This strong promise attempts to solidify the present and to preserve it in the face of contingency. This power of promise foregrounded by Arendt does not welcome the future but resists it as it seeks to preserve the raft of the present in the wake of the future.

While Arendt's view of promise seeks to secure the political accomplishments of the future and to hold the human heart to account in the future, Nietzsche focuses on the relationship of promise to the past. He discovers a special place of importance for the promise in the genealogy of the human conscience. The role of promise displays a sort of cunning reason that would extend control over the past and prevent the arrival of what is truly new. In the opening sections of the second essay of *On the Genealogy of Morality*, Nietzsche argues that a promise involves the action of memory and pain. Pain and the memory of pain is what create a promise; people are held to account if they fail. They may be subject to social or legal sanction if they fail to keep their pledges.

Despite their direction toward the future, Nietzsche points out that promises are part of the past and the way that people come to feel the force of the past in their conscience.[27] Promises are the site of the long shadow of the past, gripping the present. Taking up Nietzsche's challenge permits us to think about promise, its power, and possibility with reference to the past, with reference to origins. Failing to do so would continue the one-sided temporal insistence of the future, the privileging of the future by modern thinkers.[28]

He begins his genealogy provocatively by announcing the goal of all of morality: "To breed an animal with the prerogative to promise." Nietzsche calls this task "paradoxical" because he aims for the opposite breeding task: to breed a human being with the power of "forgetfulness," an active and powerful faculty to eliminate the past, "to shut the doors and windows . . . to make room for something new."[29] Though he aims to liberate his readers, he claims

26. Interestingly, Arendt reserves "natality" or birth for the ultimate renewal of the political, the "miracle that saves the world," which is a kind of weak power. See *The Human Condition*, pp. 246-47.

27. Arendt does refer to Nietzsche's writing on promise and demurs his failure to further develop it. *The Human Condition*, p. 245, n. 83.

28. On such a privilege of time as future, see Jürgen Habermas, *Der philosophische Diskurs der Moderne: Zwölf Vorlesungen* (Frankfurt: Suhrkamp Verlag, 1988), pp. 12-21; Stephen Kern, *The Culture of Space and Time: 1880-1917* (Cambridge: Harvard University Press, 1983), pp. 89-108; Charles Taylor, *A Secular Age* (Cambridge, MA: Belknap, 2007).

29. Friedrich Nietzsche, *On the Genealogy of Morality*, ed. Keith Ansell-Pearson, trans. Carol Diethe (Cambridge: Cambridge University Press, 2007), p. 35.

that the activity of promising stands at the head of the long trail of responsibility. Promising makes humans "peers" to one another and "predictable" because it makes each accountable to the other.[30] This history of responsibility
culminates, Nietzsche thinks, in sovereignty. The creature who embraces
promise he describes as "the sovereign individual," that "this man who is now
free, who actually has the prerogative to promise, this master of the free will,
this sovereign — how could he remain ignorant of his superiority over every-
body?" While it may seem that this sovereign individual is free, he still an-
swers to the conscience.[31] The linchpin in the construction of a person who
bears responsibility to another, the development of morality as accountability, of the sovereign kneeling before conscience, is memory. In his genealogy
of responsibility, Nietzsche holds that a "technique of mnemonics" welds
people with this sort of morality, a memory helped by pain: "When man de-
cided he had to make a memory for himself, it never happened without
blood, torments, and sacrifices."[32]

So far as one succumbs to the promise's power, one has allowed the
past reality to have force in the present. In David Hume's terms, by pointing
to a promise, the promiser is held accountable and the threat of pain or pun-
ishment applies to the one who offers the promise.[33] This may help to explain human promising in the stark terms by which Nietzsche accounts for
the development of morality, but it at least indicates the way promises are
tied up with the past as well as the future. The pledge, the offer, can be reiterated in order to hold the promiser to his or her word, to cajole, to force, to
keep the promise alive, or to bring its final delivery about. This sense of
strategy and force corresponds well with the sense of the constriction of
time and agency that Bourdieu provides in his analysis of gift-exchange even
though it embraces the past while Bourdieu primarily concerns himself with
the future.

We have gathered from Arendt and Nietzsche two pictures of promise,
both of them exhibiting a strong power. The one who can promise can master
the present in spite of anything novel; one seeks a refuge in promise in order
to shelter oneself from the contingencies of the future and the fragile settle-
ments for the present. Promise likewise controls the past, gives it life again
and again, and never welcomes the new since the recollection of the past constricts the present and future; it causes one to remember with the effect of

30. Nietzsche, *On the Genealogy of Morality*, p. 37.

31. Nietzsche, *On the Genealogy of Morality*, p. 37.

32. Nietzsche, *On the Genealogy of Morality*, p. 38.

33. David Hume, *A Treatise of Human Nature*, 2nd ed., ed. P. H. Nidditch (Oxford: Oxford University Press, 1978), pp. 524-25.

compelling one kind of action, recalling the promise to mind and shaping the present in light of that memory. In other words, promise is an exercise of power to eliminate possibility and to close off any chance for the past to be redeemed instead of being a figure that returns to haunt the present with its demands. Likewise, with the respect to Nietzsche's worry about the dominance of the past, promise is something that allows one to ignore and set the new to one side. Promise is, in its strong sense, radically inhospitable. It does not welcome the new. This does not fit the event of Pentecost. Instead, another approach must be found.

3.3. Weak Power

Pentecost could be taken to offer a promise in the strong sense. There are many traditions of interpretation which enthrone God as a sovereign in Nietzsche's sense: a God who will not welcome the new or does not risk anything in the light of the future and what may come; a God who does not expect the unexpected, whose plotlines are all set and whose intentions are sure. This God, however, is not the Triune God who acts in Pentecost, where the Spirit rests on the body of the Son to the glory of the Father. We could explore further the negative case and examine the problems that result, whether they are theological or practical, when such a God is held to be the Triune God. Instead let us articulate the positive case, the Triune God whose power is weak. As we shall see, the Icon of Pentecost gathers scripture to offer the Spirit as the event of promise, weak and hopeful.

We call this Spirit a weak power. This adjective, "weak," requires exposition. This "weak power" is a power that is open to the other, welcomes the new, and does not attempt to preserve the present in the face of the past or the future. Power is not a uniformly negative or oppressive dimension of human life. It can be creative just as it can eliminate freedom. Similar to reciprocity, it is not wise to condemn all forms of power but one needs to obtain resources to distinguish beneficial or salutary exercises of power from its negative or damaging forms.

Walter Benjamin uses the term "weak messianic power" in *On the Concept of History,* a work that poses many difficulties for the interpreter.[34] He explores the task of the thinker and her relationship to the past, culminating in

---

34. Walter Benjamin, "On the Concept of History," in *Selected Writings,* vol. 4: *1938-1940,* ed. Howard Eiland and Michael W. Jennings, trans. Edmund Jephcott et al. (Cambridge, MA: Belknap, 2003), p. 390.

a discussion of Paul Klee's painting *Angelus Novus,* which depicts an angel who is looking backward.[35] Weak power, as articulated in his theses, does not ignore the fragility of the past or present, nor does it seek to secure itself against the future. Instead, weak power firmly wishes to redeem the past from its distortions as well as to seek in the every past and present an opening for reconciliation and redemption. Benjamin aims for the exercise of weak power by a historian to uncover and find openings in every moment, openings for the Messiah to enter history through the past.[36]

Weak power in our sense means a power of the Spirit that gives the past to freedom, and that gives time and possibility where there is none. This requires us to seek out a post-metaphysical concept of possibility. To articulate a form of promise other than this strong power, we turn to the icon of Pentecost. This scene shows the descent of the Spirit in the absence of Jesus and the hope of redemption for all peoples. This puts in iconic form Jesus' farewell discourses in the Gospel of John. In John, Jesus frequently speaks of the coming Spirit, the Paraclete, as a way to keep his friends to abide in the truth in spite of Jesus' departure. His discourses attribute various tasks to the Spirit but they always talk about witness to the truth. In this way, John prepares followers of Jesus to anticipate the fragility of God in the world, a fragility that one can experience both as the truth of Jesus is disputed and contravened and as the nature of this truth itself. In summary fashion, Jesus declares: "When the Advocate comes, whom I will send to you from the Father, he will testify on my behalf" (John 15:26). Here, rather than wrenching the future to shape it to God's own will, Pentecost does not secure the Spirit or those the Spirit dwells within against the future. The friends of Jesus have no future except to dwell in the Spirit, and the Spirit's ministry returns them to the agonized torture and death of Jesus. The flesh of Jesus is the truth of God, as we frequently learn throughout the Gospel, and the flesh of Jesus is tortured and is a trial that continues although a verdict against Jesus has been issued in his crucifixion.[37]

The Spirit is the dynamism of this testing of truth. This process or forensic situation that tests the truth of God is hardly one where the strong prevail over the weak because the outcome is not yet reached. Since the followers

---

35. Benjamin, "On the Concept of History," p. 392.

36. Benjamin, "On the Concept of History," p. 397.

37. Andrew Lincoln puts it this way: "Although Jesus' own witness will have been completed and the verdict on the trial pronounced, the lawsuit continues after his departure, and in his absence there will continue to be a witness to the verdict. The witness is twofold, that of the Paraclete and that of the disciples." *Truth on Trial: The Lawsuit Motif in John's Gospel* (Grand Rapids: Baker Academic, 2000), p. 112.

of Jesus are energized by the Spirit to testify to Jesus, they share in this same agonistic trial of Jesus. Thus, to dwell in the promise of the future is neither to win out against all challenges, nor is it to preserve the past, since the past itself is disputed and under question. The crucified Jesus is himself on trial and the glory of God's only Son is on display in his wounds. This power is not strong at all, but weak to its fibers. It is, as Paul puts it, "power made perfect in weakness" (2 Cor. 12:9).

While the strong version of promise resists the new by failing to give to the other, by only preserving memory in order to dominate and subordinate the new, Pentecost is a promise to another and so the gift of the Spirit is a gift of God's glory and a giving up of any reservation of power. Thus, outpouring is indeed pouring out the Spirit without reserve. The promise of the Spirit places, as it were, God in this trial. God, by so promising and so giving the Spirit, allows the Spirit to enter into immanent exchanges and the give and take of the trial of truth, in the terms of the Gospel of John. Compare this to Nietzsche, for whom welcoming the new requires a kind of radical amnesia.

Bringing this discussion of power back into discussions of promise and gift, we can see that the agency of the Spirit as a doubled and extended gift directs the community of Jesus' friends in two directions. The Spirit witnesses to Jesus and points forward to the fulfillment of Jesus' trial, the disclosure to the whole cosmos that God's truth is the man Jesus. Thus, Pentecost is a gift that is inserted in reference to the given, to what comes before its advent, and it also points toward the full gift of the Spirit. Indeed, one might take the constant refrain of "abiding" or "remaining" in God as the way in which Pentecost welcomes the new from the future and seeks redemption of the past. The future and past of this Spirit is the one to whom the witness is directed: the truth is in flesh, is the truth of the tortured Jesus. Those who love, those who are Jesus' friends, those who testify to the truth of Jesus' crucifixion: all these are those in whom the Spirit abides. Abiding in this trial as a witness is a kind of agency and relationship to time that prioritizes the possible and welcomes the new while redeeming the past. This sort of redemption of the past can be the weak power that Benjamin points out and a weak power that distinguishes the promise of the Spirit from that strong power exercised on behalf of the political in Arendt's conception.

We may hold that Pentecost gives time in the sense that the descent of the Spirit allows for communities, people, and the whole cosmos to testify to the truth of Jesus, a truth which is in dispute and under examination. The Spirit grants this possibility to dwell in the place of Jesus' body and therefore in the midst of this trial in order to hope that God's truth in the world indeed is this crucified form. This means that the Spirit descends to give a new relationship to the past as it gives participation in Jesus himself. When this event falls onto the church, it allows the church to consider the body of Jesus in other ways than as he may seem: a failed Messiah, a teacher of impossible commandments, a figure whose love gathers a community rife with the unfaithful and marked by betrayal. Benjamin writes in *On the Concept of History* that the relationship to the past is to recover in it what has been lost or obscured in history. This means the truth to which the Spirit witnesses is the cross of Jesus. This is what it means for the eternal Spirit to rest on the body of the Son, for the Spirit to be the future of God's very being.[38]

The singular, crucified Jesus opens other places to be seen as multiple Golgothas. Because the Spirit further and further offers a chance to abide in that Jesus, this dwelling allows us to consider and open up how all other pasts are buried and open. The past can continue to pain the present. The Spirit who descends at Pentecost, by offering the possibility to witness to the truth of the given, allows us to sort out the distortions, wounds, and omissions that mar our relationship to the past. Since the Spirit offers a weak power it does not continue the past into the future; it has a critical relationship to the present and the past. It seeks to open up blocked possibilities buried in the past and to offer a chance for redemption. This means to give time in the sense to free up the burden of the past.

Pentecost can offer this critical relationship to the past since it offers possibility, which addresses Nietzsche's concern that it valorizes the past at the expense of the new. Clearly, conflict over the role of the given and its authority or power in the present has vexed hermeneutics. Without recounting the many twists of the role of the given, suffice it to say that any critical relationship to the past cannot accept what is given, what appears simply as such. The outpouring of the Spirit witnesses to the truth of Jesus and so asks us to reconsider the body of Jesus, to take again what is given to us. The power of the Spirit, who searches the depths of all things, including the depths of God, is to open up not only the unrealized and forgotten pasts, but to allow the past to be other than what it is. In the Spirit, the tortured body of Christ is both the failure of love and its accomplishment; the possibility the Spirit brings to the body of Christ we ordinarily call resurrection. The outpouring of the Spirit onto the present and the past does not simply endorse the given and accept the state of affairs that we accept as a reality common to us. But it would not simply abandon them or negate the given in full. In discerning the pres-

---

38. Robert W. Jenson offers the necessary outline of the Spirit's personhood as an agent over-and-against the Father and the Son in *Systematic Theology*, vol. 1 (Oxford: Oxford University Press, 1997), p. 160.

ent in the dwelling Spirit, a community is enjoined to the possibilities of what things are and the state of affairs that may be. This is to encourage a sort of ordinary possibility, to help things along and nurture them to be what they could be. But it is also to uncover and enable discarded possibilities and to unearth what never was or could never be, to present not only what was once possible but to embrace what is entirely impossible.

3.4. Possibility

The weak power of the Spirit in Pentecost gives us a way to articulate the post-metaphysical concept of possibility at work in promise. Because we are able to think about the way that power is exercised, we can so delineate the being of the promise and then use that concept of possibility to discuss the agency of creatures who dwell in the promise. The possibility that the Spirit brings in its promise is a possibility that not only enjoins what could have been but also what is not and never was. This possibility bridges both what one might ordinarily mean when one intends by *possibility* the meanings of "could" or "perhaps" but also what counts as "impossibility." As we have seen, Pentecost is the event wherein God promises the Spirit, giving the Spirit first and then promising its fulfillment. This promising is the gift of possibility, the giving of possibility to another, the gift of time.

As we have seen, promise as gift exceeds the ordinary sense of cause and effect since it is neither a something nor a nothing and so cannot be understood to offer possibility in a sense that is derivative from some actuality. In this search we seek in possibility, potentiality, or in becoming a way to unveil the being of God or of creation in light of God's gifts in a way more true to God as a lover, as a lavish giver, as a creative yet beneficent power whose sign is the hanged man of Golgotha, whose future is the future of the Spirit. For instance, Eberhard Jüngel and Oswald Bayer alike note that the powerful central insistence of Martin Luther on the justification of the ungodly *(iustificatio impii),* the righteousness of the unfaithful, demands a radical reorientation of God's actions and power if God prefers and creates righteousness where none is.[39] Both Jüngel and Robert W. Jenson construct postmetaphysical concepts of being and possibility for God precisely because they

---

39. Eberhard Jüngel, "Die Welt als Möglichkeit und Wirklichkeit: Zum ontologischen Ansatz der Rechtfertigungslehre," in *Unterwegs zur Sache,* 3rd ed. (Tübingen: Mohr Siebeck, 2000), pp. 206-33; Oswald Bayer, "Rechtfertigungslehre und Ontologie," in *Zugesagte Gegenwart* (Tübingen: Mohr Siebeck, 2007), pp. 196-205.

hold that possibility is not subordinate to actuality in God's being.[40] A metaphysical account, here, means a concept of being that always ties possibility to actuality, taking possibility always to be a lesser and inferior kind of being that is eliminated when actuality comes. Though these proposals seem to depart from or challenge traditional and metaphysical accounts of God's being, they have the benefit of leading the way for our work. In many ways this problem parallels the questions that have long confronted Christian theological tradition's wrestling with how best to construct a doctrine of creation — for, as everyone knows, nothing will come of nothing.

The power of the Spirit, as I have introduced in considering the various texts organized by the icon of Pentecost, has a temporal dimension that reaches intimately into the past while also opening up the future to what may come. The future is not a settled place from which the Spirit blows — instead the Spirit is the future, a welcome that allows one to expect the unexpected. To insist otherwise would subordinate the Spirit to time rather than see it as the Spirit's own offering. To embrace possibility as the primary mode of the Spirit's existence does not mean that we privilege futurity over the past; it does not mean that novelty and the new somehow neglects the old. The old king at the center of the assembled church in the icon waits for redemption and longs for what is to come; the Spirit will not leave him and the peoples he represents behind. To so privilege the future in spite of the past would neglect the relationship that promise has with the given, with the gift of creation. Thus, to utilize the language of time, the future reaches to the past and gives it new light; it does not simply abolish or purely negate what has come before now. It negates this past while transforming and revisiting it.

The interrelationships between time, power, and promise that we have developed in our analysis of the icon of Pentecost and its companions in Scripture require us to discuss them in terms of their being, and in terms of their possibility. Giving time means giving possibility to another in the various modes we have outlined. So giving possibility is giving a particular mode of being.

In many metaphysical and post-metaphysical writings, possibility derives from actuality.[41] Though this claim usually requires a substantive definition or discussion of what counts as actual being or reality, in general possi-

---

40. Eberhard Jüngel, *Gott als Geheimnis der Welt: Zur Begründung der Theologie des Gekreuzigten im Streit zwischen Theismus und Atheismus* (Tübingen: Mohr Siebeck, 1977), pp. 1-43, 505-43; Jenson, *Systematic Theology,* vol. 1, pp. 207-23.

41. Eberhard Jüngel summarizes this problem in "Die Welt als Möglichkeit und Wirklichkeit," pp. 208-11.

bility denotes that which could be, might have been, or some state of affairs other than what is, was, or will be. In other senses, possibility simply contrasts something that is contingent from that which is necessary; it shows what could be different in contrast to that which cannot be otherwise than what it is. Nevertheless, the possible is a lesser reality in these schemes than an actual one, not even to say a necessary one. This means that something is possible if it might have actuality but does not presently, which is to say that to speak of possibility only in the future tense, to consider possibility to be a feature of temporality. Or it might consider possibility to say that something else in the past could have occurred differently, to recognize that the events of the past are not the only way such events could have progressed.[42] Both of these subordinate possibility to what is or what was.

These ways of constructing possibility are defined by actuality as presence. Martin Heidegger defines metaphysics as that discipline which defines being as that which is present.[43] Just so, metaphysical concepts of possibility are not present to consciousness; this possibility does not appear since it does not take up space, nor does it harden into events and things. Possibility qualifies as an impoverished phenomenon since it has no analogy to an object or thing. Many dispute to which thinkers this definition applies, but if metaphysics is defined as that way of thinking that is stuck on according reality to those things that have presence, that way of thinking that only grants the name "real" to that which appears and presents itself to a knowing conscience as a phenomenon, takes up time and space, has spatial extension, and other features that determine presence, then possibility always is this shade of actuality, and is somehow that lesser being or is granted a kind of quasi-reality between nothing and something. And so it may seem that a metaphysical definition of possibility can characterize the being of promise. When we took up the strangers' promise to Sarah and Abraham in the last chapter, we noted that the promise they offer as a counter-gift hovers between those two poles of something and nothing; we could also consider that this promise that they offer is both nothing and utterly beyond being. But since the promise enters into the give-and-take of an archaic gift economy in a way that both leaps over and glides underneath the cause-and-effect of the circle that those gifts travel, a promise has being in the realm of the possible. It is both nothing and something.

42. Richard Kearney distinguishes three kinds of possibility in metaphysical thought. We refer to only two of them. See Richard Kearney, *The God Who May Be: The Hermeneutics of Religion* (Bloomington: Indiana University Press, 2001), pp. 80-100.

43. For an excellent summary of Heidegger's description of metaphysics, see Jean-François Courtine, *Inventio analogiae: Métaphysique et ontothéologie* (Paris: Vrin, 2005), pp. 45-82.

The power of the Spirit does not fit a metaphysical scheme. As we have seen, the event of Pentecost introduces the past and the future in ways that defy this metaphysics of presence. If the Spirit returns us to a past which the world disputes, as framed by the Gospel of John, and asks us to take this rejected body as the truth of the cosmos and of God, then we are introduced to a nothing, a nobody, an impossibility in the person of Jesus. This non-person is the event Pentecost promises. Jesus is both our past and future, since Pentecost is a promise of this Spirit who returns us to the crucified Jesus as well as wrenching us to expect his future.

There are many post-metaphysical constructions of being. These are developed to fit many different purposes, some of which are antithetical to a theological analysis of gift. We shall proceed through our analysis of promise in conjunction with time and power. Since promise is a weak power, we shall need to consider how giving and power relate in ways alternate to Bourdieu's construal of gift-exchange as a means by which parties gain power over one another.

Giorgio Agamben provides the question of possibility to that of power that will allow us to differentiate the kind of possibility given by promise from other sorts.[44] He has provided a way to consider possibility and power together through his analysis of sovereignty, a kind of power exercised in the political sphere: sovereignty usually belongs to the kind of strong power that Arendt and Nietzsche consider. Indeed, Nietzsche considers the sort of power exercised by promise to have resulted in the figure of the sovereign. Agamben considers the problem of sovereignty that is staged for him by Carl Schmitt. Schmitt, a German jurist and philosopher of the Weimar and National Socialist eras, argues that a political sovereign, even if that sovereign is elected through democratic procedures, has the power to outstrip the constitutionally prescribed limits to his or her power when facing an exceptional situation. Since a truly exceptional situation is one that no one has expected or could expect, the provision for exceptional acts allows the sovereign to decide the exception, in Schmitt's terms. While Schmitt's account of political power is highly contested and perhaps is checked in practice by all sorts of dimensions of civil society and informal institutions, Agamben argues that the problems that face political power in this sense of sovereignty are problems that have to be confronted. He claims that human life always faces the excess of sovereignty since the unexpected, the stranger, and the marginal always

<hr />

44. I have examined Giorgio Agamben and Carl Schmitt in greater detail in Gregory Walter, "Critique and Promise in Paul Tillich's Political Theology: Engaging Giorgio Agamben on Sovereignty and Possibility," *Journal of Religion* 90 (2010): 458-62.

need to be tamed, domesticated, blunted, and forced to fit the categories of one's understanding or the laws which govern the body; failing that, the stranger should be exiled or killed. Possibility represents the new or strange that can upset already existing relationships and situations. And so in the guise of protecting the ordinary, the sovereign may practice rejection rather than acceptance in order to maintain power. Promise can be recruited in order to sustain this view so long as promise exists as a strong power in the sense that Arendt articulates.

Agamben articulates a post-metaphysical concept of possibility that represents the figure of the absolute sovereign; in a theological sense, the God of strong power. He clearly differentiates his sense of possibility severed from actuality. He makes use of Aristotle's concept of possibility articulated in his *De Anima*.[45] This sovereign, who "decides the exception," exercises power in a way that the sovereign can not only act in an ordinary sense but also may act exceptionally, in new ways, in surprising ways to meet that unexpected state of affairs called the state of exception. The sovereign is one who gives possibility to himself and himself alone and so is able to anticipate that which a person cannot anticipate by always refusing actuality to that exceptional state. A sort of pure possibility exists in the condition of absolute sovereignty that consists of a possibility that would never bow to the hard and fast coming-to-be of actuality. Since sovereignty is that which exceeds the ordinary, the determinate, the actual, sovereign power in Agamben's analysis is power that never allows itself to have limits or constraints. Thus, it is always a potency that gives itself to itself and therefore absorbs all actuality into itself.

Agamben claims that this kind of pure possibility deals with the unexpected by turning it into possibility; in other words, the sovereign can liquidate all that is actual into possibility. In practical terms, this is to turn life into death, which is why Agamben calls any politics that deals with the exceptional in this way "thanatopolitics." Thus, everything and everyone may be negated, rejected, or killed despite their rights as citizens or international status. Likewise, the sovereign, when exercising this exceptional power, does not need to account for it. The nature of the exceptional exercise of power does not give itself as actuality and so never appears, never reaches any hard and fast position whereby one could call the sovereign into question. Sovereignty is a way for those who exercise it to escape all publicity and accountability because it

45. Agamben also articulates this in the essay "On Potentiality," in *Potentialities: Collected Essays in Philosophy*, ed. and trans. Daniel Heller-Roazen (Stanford: Stanford University Press, 1999), pp. 177-84. He later repeats many of these claims in discussion of sovereignty in *Homo Sacer: Sovereign Power and Bare Life*, trans. Daniel Heller-Roazen (Stanford: Stanford University Press, 1998), pp. 44-48. See Walter, "Critique and Promise," pp. 459-62.

is a construal of power that is always a gift of itself to itself. This power is not weak, and is not oriented to the other, as promise is.

The kind of power that Agamben outlines from Schmitt allows us to more carefully construct the kind of possibility evident in the weak power of Pentecost. The Spirit promises and so gives possibility to another. This gift of possibility that is the Spirit's very self is a possibility that embraces otherness, which awaits the future. This marks the fundamental difference between sovereign power and its inability to welcome the new or to resurrect the past. The Spirit is not without sovereignty altogether, utterly divested of any power. Rather, the Spirit is otherwise than sovereign by giving Spirit to another.

By reaching into the past and offering Jesus' righteousness, by binding together events, things, and communities to the crucified Jesus, promise gives possibility to another in contrast to the giving of possibility to one's self, in making the impossible possible. By holding open this door in the past and the future, the Spirit allows for a possibility and agency of the other. This is the other-driven aim of the Spirit — to include others in the life of the Triune God, along with the Spirit being the very gift that God gives. Rather than reserving the gift of possibility and therefore actuality for oneself, as Agamben's sovereign does, the Spirit gives nothing other than the Spirit's self to another, giving possibility to the other. It does so by the same structure of the phenomena of promise as before: through its doubling and extension. It should be noted that the initial gift is and is not; it is somewhere between nothing and actuality and so a promise, while it is not yet fulfilled, is always possibility.

This possibility is given by participation in the Spirit. To give possibility as Pentecost does is not merely to give a relation exterior to the recipient. This does not leave the one on whom the Spirit rests unchanged and merely give a new point of reference. It is to offer participation in the Spirit and therefore in the Triune God. This resting is a dwelling, an opening that is given to unblock the closed possibilities of the past and to allow individuals and communities to act in novel ways and to risk what seems impossible. This means that the promise is a gift to another; it gives the gift of action, of possibility to another, and so opens up a field of action, the field of love.

But we can also articulate the possibility of promise in the sense of its credibility. Promise is possible so far as it is trusted. The promised reality may come about in some sense without that trust, but as a possibility engaged in and available it is only a possibility so far as it is believed. The promise requires this credit since it is a self-dispossessing act of the Spirit. To put it another way, promise, by giving possibility to another, allows for the exception, the extraordinary, the strange, to give judgment on the one promising. This means that to receive the promise, the gift of time, is to receive a possibility

58

that is not already given within the drifts and momentums currently at work in one's life. It is to see a new breath given; the wells of this possibility are granted to the blocked chances of the past, to revisit with hope the horrors of the slain as well as to welcome the arrival of the strange. This possibility is not available in the sense of mastery but is available in the wake of a doubled gift; it is to be dwelt in and not possessed.

3.5. *Arrabon*

The remaining feature of strong power in the promise is the idea that Bourdieu presents, that the delay of a promise, that its giving and never returning is actually a strategy that the one promising uses in order to keep power over the other by failing to issue any resolution to the promise. If I promise but always hold off on fulfilling that promise, I can either continually lose credibility or be simply leading the recipient on, keeping her in line. We can carry this out in terms of the truth of God that the Spirit articulates. If the truth of God is disputed and under trial, this truth has an eschatological nature since its outcome is forthcoming, underway, and awaiting a final resolution. The truth of the Spirit is promissory in nature since the farewell discourse of John finds Jesus stating that the Spirit will bring the world into the fullness of truth. This means that the final adjudication of what God's truth is and its relationship to Jesus' trial is anticipatory upon the final gift of the Spirit, the same gift that we are given in Pentecost since the Spirit gives no other gift than Spirit. Though we surely need to develop this sense of truth more, our goal here is more modest, to articulate Pentecost as a weak power and consider the difficulties placed upon such a promise.

If the truth of Jesus and the work of the Spirit assume this structure, exercise this power, and give time in this way, Pentecost is a promise, that is, is a doubled and extended gift. We have seen that what is given in Pentecost is itself weak and fails to preserve the present or embalm the past; rather, it affords possibility in all cases. But the delay of what is promised, the wait instantiated in order to fulfill the promise, could be a strategy in Bourdieu's sense, an effort to dominate or oppress. Likewise, Derrida points out a significant difficulty with promise: once fulfilled, the promise is concluded. A promise is fundamentally open, creates expectation and desire for its arrival and conclusion. To consider the act of promise complete is one of the weaknesses in speech-act theory pointed out by Derrida.[46] To articulate this weak

46. See Chapter 1, above, section 3, "Speech-Act and Promise."

power in another, we also invoke the antinomy of hope. Robert W. Jenson puts this forward as a central problem of the eschatologically-driven theologies that descend from the dialectical theologians of the Weimar era. If one promises a future, what happens to that promise when it arrives? Or, in the terms of human hope, does the arrival of that in which we hope or the state-of-affairs that are hoped for mean that hope is now useless? Rather, promise extends the future into the present as *arrabon* or down payment of the Reign of God even while the end is constantly arriving.[47]

The promise of the Spirit, where the down payment and the end promise is the same, is to receive again or in full what one already has. When Jesus first speaks of the comforter in John's gospel, he speaks of the gift of the Spirit "without measure." Robert W. Jenson puts it in this way: "Hope ceases when what is hoped for arrives. Must not the Kingdom, in which all hope is fulfilled, be then the entire cessation of hope, and so death and not life?"[48] Living by promise and so by faith would only be then a temporary matter. The life of freedom engendered by the promise, a gift that creates no debt or obligation, would then finally arrive and so indebt its recipients. If I promise and finally deliver on that promise, I have given an ordinary, archaic gift. All the anticipation of its fulfillment would be washed away into the past as such a gift would exert its force and demand a counter-gift, and uphold the circle of ordinary exchange.

One solution would be to consider a promissory form of Derrida's construction of expectation that never arrives.[49] But a promise like that would be ultimately a negative endeavor, an an-iconic stance that would resist even the description of Pentecost that the icon gives. Promise would cease to be a doubled and extended gift since it would be identical to the pure gift that never arrives.

Instead, promise as a weak power has a future: the gift given in the future, according to the icon, is the future of Jesus, the measureless gift that is the Spirit. Though this essay has focused on developing a phenomenology of promise and has not developed its concept of promise in relationship to Trinitarian doctrine and tradition, that kind of reasoning can now become more explicit.

47. On *arrabon* in Paul's writing, see Kurt Erlemann, "Der Geist als *arrabon* (2Kor 5,5) im Kontext der paulinischen Eschatologie," *Zeitschrift für die neutestamentliche Wissenschaft und die Kunde des Urchristentums* 83 (1992): 202-23.

48. Jenson, *Systematic Theology*, vol. 1, p. 198.

49. This is best summarized by John D. Caputo under the heading of "the messianic" in Derrida. See Caputo, ed., *Deconstruction in a Nutshell: A Conversation with Jacques Derrida* (New York: Fordham University Press, 1997), pp. 156-80.

If something came after the gift of the Spirit, that God would send another, then that promise would be succeeded by yet another and so the Spirit would not be God. Likewise, the Spirit's gift is not sheer persistence, whether it is sculpted into eternity as the permanent arrival of the promise or as constant anticipation. Jenson puts these reasons clearly:

> The future brought by the Spirit — whether to the Father or now in the church or as the Kingdom — is determinate as the triumph of Jesus, and so a describable state of affairs. But what of when it arrives? Does another future open after it? Then the Spirit is not God. Or does it thereafter timelessly persist? Then God is not the biblical God.[50]

God's promise is a promise of the Spirit and so is not finished though it may arrive. The double bind that Derrida points out shows how Pentecost as an event of promise differs from other phenomena: a promise must be fulfilled in order to be a promise, but once a promise arrives, it is concluded. Thus, a promise that is fulfilled without conclusion such as that of Pentecost is perhaps finally the only promise worthy of the name.

Yet, the antinomy of hope is the same as the antinomy of the Spirit. Jenson articulates the way forward in terms of love:

> Love is a state of affairs, a particular relation among specific persons. [. . .] The coming of love is an event that can occur and be followed by no other, without thereby compelling the lovers to cling to something finished and merely enduring. For love is itself openness to unbounded possibility.[51]

If what Pentecost promises is the Spirit, a gift of possibility, this gift persists without ceasing to be lively and continues without ceasing. There is nothing after Pentecost in any sense, for all is dwelling in the promise.

As we return to the icon of Pentecost, the event of promise, we see that not only does the descent of the Spirit give time and possibility. It also gives place and orients for action. It interrupts the present while returning us to the peoples who wait in the center of the assembly. Though it does these things, they all occur weakly, as a fragile web that befits the power of the Spirit.

50. Jenson, *Systematic Theology,* vol. 1, p. 219.
51. Jenson, *Systematic Theology,* vol. 1, p. 220.

CHAPTER 4

The Impure Gift

Dixi, quae feurit tentatio Abrahae, nempe contradictio promissionis.

Martin Luther, *Vorlesungen über 1. Mose* (1535-45)

Promise, as a doubled and extended gift, whets our appetite and enacts a desire for its future. But in the meantime this promise is a gift, after all, one that is wholly given for our sake and lacks any condition. Just so, it interrupts us and through us it can interrupt the distortions of this life, calling attention to the fractures and injuries that we experience. We do not pass the promise on to others — we await its coming. But by interrupting ourselves with our others, our immediate world, our locale, our neighborhood, we can attend to injury and the impurity of our giving and receiving. The promise frees us through this interruption even as we await freedom in the arrival of the promise.

The other way to put this practical orientation is that when promise gives possibility, it offers a place for action toward the self and the other. The possibility the Spirit grants is the possibility the Spirit is, directed toward the other. I shall consider this action as a moral act, the recognition of the neighbor. The practical or moral effect of dwelling in God's promise allows one to interrupt destructive social exchanges as well as to offer other gifts, ones desperately needed, and to offer them in their impurity. Where advocates of the pure and reciprocal gift expect the span that obtains between gift and counter-gift to be merely a field of anticipation for action, God's promise creates a ground fertile for the welling up of love. This field affords action that liberates creatures in order to rightly perceive the demands of neighbors in the many other economies that press upon them.

The fundamental difference between taking promise as an orientation and the other uses of gift is that promise enables recognition of the neighbor as well as criticism of existing gift economies and the given rather than continuing, fulfilling, or transforming them.[1] Since a promise is a doubled and extended gift, it resolves this problem of continuing the gift by showing how trusting gives a gift back to God and that giving onward to the neighbor (or receiving) occurs in the immanent sphere of creation, all the rivers and streams of everyday life that flow in and out of one's immediate place of responsibility. Every act within promise simultaneously emerges from the trust of the promise given, its present token, as well as anticipation of the promise's fulfillment.

The interruption that this promise brings seems to be the pure gift and therefore it would forever glance alongside the ordinary cycles of giving, the regular demands and give-and-take of life. On the contrary, to live from promise allows creatures to encounter impure giving and to recognize their failings in order to rightly serve themselves and the neighbor. But this difference between promise and the repeated gift further permits a plurality of God's actions and allows us to properly take into account that crucial disaster of divinity, where God undermines or opposes God's own promise. The Binding of Isaac has been a text where sacrifice, gift, and God have intersected for many writers. As we shall see, it is a place where nothing less occurs than God contradicting God's promise. Such a situation demands an account of promise that allows for a more plural depiction of God's actions.

In order to demonstrate the orientation of practice that wells up in promise, I shall show how the promise takes up the interruptive and critical possibilities of the pure gift and how the promise is itself a place for the exchange of other gifts. This requires attending to a common effort of theological adoption of the gift: to consider the gift given by God and the one given in turn by Christians to be part of one concatenation of giving. In this scheme it could be one continuous gift repeated, or a unilateral gift that is disseminated with abandon, without reason, and without return. Though the theologians who do develop this gift argue that there is a fundamental difference between

---

1. I use *orientation* here in two senses. The first is that promise affords a direction within all of the existing economies, demands, and needs that press upon individuals. The second is to suggest the main directions that practical or ethical action is given in schematic terms but not in full. Even though the weak promise does not give the kind of strong version of orientation that Kant employs, it aims lower and gives a kind of a direction to the other. On Kant's view of orientation, see Immanuel Kant, "What Does It Mean to Orient Oneself in Thinking?" in *Religion and Rational Theology*, ed. and trans. Allen W. Wood and George Di Giovanni (Cambridge: Cambridge University Press, 1996), p. 8.

God's giving and human or immanent gifts, the point at question here is how the acts of these two different agents fit together.

4.1. Gift and Morality

The gift has always stood close to moral reflection and practical imperatives. This intimate relationship readily appears in the role of reciprocity as an imperative to give. In archaic giving, the gift goes on to demand a counter-gift whose continuance has no end even when it returns to the original giver. The action of any person within this field of gift-exchange is constrained by the appearance of that gift. When put into a general scheme, this kind of giving and its obligations can easily shift from descriptive to normative claims for action. Most theological adoptions of gift-giving do not overlook the practical significance of gift-exchange for developing theological ethics and poetics. Indeed, Marcel Mauss's epoch-making study on the gift concludes with a final chapter devoted to a moral program meant to revive gift-economy in his society, offering numerous observations about how societies, informal groups, civil society, and industries might develop greater humanity and solidarity by embracing the moral vision that archaic giving offers. He proposes a society that reestablishes lost solidarity between citizens, workers and employers, families and the public.[2] He suggests the resurrection of gift-exchange could serve as a moral norm to guide social welfare generally, summarizing his hopes for a just society in a proverb: "Give as much as you take, and all will be well."[3] Others have amended this program, taking stock of the many features of modern social life that differ from the archaic cultures that define the gift, such as the role of honor, the character of public actions, and the idea of human agency.[4]

The promise itself is not reciprocal but enables reciprocity. Since there is a fine line between gifts that poison and those that benefit, Paul Ricoeur has stressed the critical importance of discerning beneficial and damaging reciprocity.[5] If promise is to involve itself in reciprocity in any fashion, it should provide resources to allow its recipients to reject or correct instances

2. Marcel Mauss, *The Gift: The Form and Reason for Exchange in Archaic Society,* trans. W. D. Halls (New York: Norton, 1990), pp. 78-83.

3. Mauss, *The Gift,* p. 71.

4. In particular Jacques T. Goudbout with Alain Caillé, *The World of the Gift,* trans. Donald Winkler (Montreal: McGill-Queen's University Press, 1998).

5. Paul Ricoeur, *Parcours de la reconnaissance: Trois études* (Paris: Gallimard, 2001), pp. 374-77.

of bad reciprocity and to engage in just gift-exchanges. Thus, any discussion of the moral dimension of gift-giving requires publicity, or an arena wherein gifts can be tested and acts of recognition weighed in order to judge their equity and justice.

Similarly, Pierre Bourdieu and Jacques Derrida have reiterated older concerns about the gift, such as how a giver can use a gift to hold power over another, or that the gift's force creates unwelcome social relationships. In short, one of the reasons Derrida holds out hope for a gift purified of all exchange is to trade on the impossible gift that benefits without binding. Promise does not succumb to some of Derrida's and Bourdieu's criticisms of a reciprocal gift in previous chapters.[6] But Derrida also has considered how the gift in his pure sense would engender action, how it might even be given. Few follow Derrida in his entirety, but many take him as a general marker of the outer-limits of gift-giving.[7]

Finally, Marcel Hénaff and Paul Ricoeur have made the most significant advance to discuss the practical importance of the gift. They have shown how gift-exchange is essential to the moral process known as recognition.[8] Gift-giving is the way that one recognizes another. The exchange of gifts establishes otherness and permits the mutual recognition of each other, according not only the proper social standing but allowing for attention to the material needs of life along with social goods. As we shall see, recognition is not altogether a pure act. Though the term signifies a broad range of relationships and actions that hold great importance in our pluralist society, where the negotiation of differences of many kinds matters in everyday life, we shall find that recognition is most usually misrecognition and so perhaps the most important practical act of responsibility that we may take while dwelling in promise is that of solidarity and repentance.

However, we first need to show that a promise enables giving, recognition, and action though it itself is not handed on. This requires attention to

6. See Chapter 2 above for Derrida, Chapter 3 for Bourdieu.

7. Alongside the powerful accounts of Derrida in John Caputo, *The Prayers and Tears of Jacques Derrida: Religion without Religion* (Bloomington: Indiana University Press, 1997), pp. 161-211, consider Caputo's adaptation and expansion of this pure gift in the mode of forgiveness and hospitality in *The Weakness of God: A Theology of the Event* (Bloomington: Indiana University Press, 2006), pp. 208-35, 259-78. Stephen Webb has also offered a Trinitarian adaptation of Derrida's gift in *The Gifting God: A Trinitarian Ethics of Excess* (Oxford: Oxford University Press, 1996).

8. Marcel Hénaff, *The Price of Truth: Gift, Money, and Philosophy*, trans. Jean-Louis Morhange (Stanford: Stanford University Press, 2010), pp. 395-404; Ricoeur, *Parcours de reconnaissance*, pp. 373-77.

interruption and how the promise is the well of the event of freedom, dwelling in the possibility-given-to-another that is the Spirit.

4.2. Repeating God's Gift

To return the gift is the last of obligations Mauss outlined. This last obligation is the third and final node of the circular, reciprocated gift.[9] If promise enables giving in a beneficial and critical sense, it will be able to effect gift-exchange and agency.

Similarly, Kathryn Tanner holds that God's gifts engender individual givers, though without relation and without continuance.[10] Though promise does enable giving and receiving without itself being continued, it does not eschew relation or require the kind of giving-at-a-distance or anonymity that Tanner holds necessary to preserve the unconditional character of the gift she advocates. Promise, as we shall see, requires a careful consideration of what is beneficial and needful in exchange and so there must be a back-and-forth between giver and recipient. Tanner's construction of gift as charity without relation cannot sustain that need because it lacks this mutual engagement.[11]

But the gift must be surprising as well. Following Derrida and his reading of gift in several theologians, Stephen Webb holds that God's excessive gift is uncontrolled when handed on by givers.[12] What unites the reception of God's gift and the turn to give to others is human gratitude. Of course, in each of these cases there is a Christological claim that links and permits such giving despite human bondage to sin, which, in a theology governed by discourse on the gift, considers sin as the refusal of God's gifts. Promise enables giving without itself being repeated or continued on in the manner of the archaic gift.

Martin Luther can stand in for many to demonstrate how it may seem that divine gifts continue on in further giving. He writes:

---

9. Mauss, *The Gift*, pp. 13-14.

10. Kathryn Tanner, *Economy of Grace* (Minneapolis: Fortress Press, 2005), pp. 63-65.

11. Tanner develops the non-obligatory response of gratitude in conversation with Paul F. Camenisch, "Gift and Gratitude in Ethics," *The Journal of Religious Ethics* 9 (1981): 1-34. However, Camenisch does not eschew mutuality or the social relation. For gratitude to free up the individual participants from obligation in gift-exchange, there must be reciprocity agreed upon by all participants. Tanner's anonymous giving and giving-at-a-distance does not permit this.

12. Webb, *The Gifting God*, p. 154.

This teaching [on Christian freedom] tells us that the good we have from God should flow from one to the other and be common to all. Everyone should "put on" the neighbor and act toward him or her as if we were in the neighbor's place. The good that flowed from Christ flows into us. Christ has "put on" us and acted for us as if he had been what we are. The good we receive from Christ flows from us toward those who have need of it.[13]

Luther's view of the gift appears straightforwardly archaic: the gifts that come from Christ are given to us and then, in turn, we pass them on to others. One chain occurring in this text allows the good to flow in a roughly analogous way through the various nodes of Christ, self, and neighbor. The pattern for giving the gift on to others and so to recognize others would occur under the sign of repetition, as pointed out by Milbank.[14] For him, the point of any giving or act subsequent to the reception of God's gift is to repeat it differently. To repeat differently, rather than to merely repeat, is to attend to the analogous character of God's gifts as well as their multiplicity. The gift needs to be surprising in order to prevent it from being fit to the iron laws of reciprocity but the gift must also be genuinely needed by the recipient in order for the gift to be appropriate and not an alien force that will impose itself.[15]

However, Luther's text points toward the interaction of two sets of exchanges instead of one that is continuous and overarching, beginning with God and ending with human action. Here, gift occurs in two different segments. This exchange requires more than just the giving of something, in Luther's position, since it requires the giver to "take on" the neighbor. There is not just a one-way exchange of passing along goods but also a reverse motion of reception. Givers here are not givers who never receive, but duly receive another's place.

The Christian's act is enabled by Christ. As Luther has argued throughout *The Freedom of a Christian,* this kind of giving occurs dynamically on account of participation in Jesus himself. This is Luther's famous "happy exchange," where Jesus gives his righteousness and takes on sin. He summarizes it in the conclusion of the work: "As Christians we do not live in ourselves but we live in Christ through faith and in the neighbor through love."[16] Luther also

13. Martin Luther, *Freedom of a Christian,* trans. Mark Tranvik (Minneapolis: Fortress Press, 2006), p. 88.

14. Most significantly in John Milbank, "Can a Gift Be Given? Prolegomena to a Future Trinitarian Metaphysic," *Modern Theology* 11 (1995): 124-26.

15. John Milbank, "The Transcendentality of the Gift: A Summary," in *The Future of Love: Essays in Political Theology* (Eugene: Cascade Books, 2009), p. 357.

16. Luther, *Freedom of a Christian,* p. 88.

adds a directional emphasis in these two participations, these two directions of gift. Through faith we are caught up beyond ourselves into God. Likewise, we descend below to dwell in our neighbor. These directional metaphors reproduce the Christological moments in ordinary human giving. Descent does not refer to social standing but a directional depiction of the incarnation of the logos. Similarly, the exchange that Luther describes is an exchange that he describes as the transition from death to life. Participation in Christ, which is being bound to Christ, radically transforms, indeed interrupts the individual in a significant way. This is another bar against the gift of Christ being handed on in an untroubled way by the individual Christian.

Repetition requires delay in order for it to be repetition and not mere continuance.[17] But promise is extended, not repeated; if there were time, a delay that obtained after promise, this would not be the promise of the Spirit.[18] Any repetition would occur within it and so the promise as a whole is not repeated. This further means that all action occurs within the promise, between its initial token and its fulfillment. Action between or within the promise is therefore anticipatory of the promise and a reorientation living from the initial token rather than a continuance or a transfer of the gift.[19] It does not repeat differently, to use Milbank's phrase for his purified gift, but rather, action occurs within the promise, during its extension.

This promise, if thought of as a continuous gift, fails to interact with the already-existing world into which it is introduced. The hope that the continuous gift will bear practical fruit can give it much credence. But promise can afford a critical impulse as well as an expectation of fulfillment of already existing economies, gifts, and demands that are occurring. Since the promise enters into this plurality of voices, actions, impoverishment, and riches, it affords action in that sphere rather than a continuance of the initial gift.

To show how this interruption and recognition occur, we must return again to the general form of promise. If the one promised has anything when she has a promise, she has something that is and is not. This can hardly be passed or repeated in any ordinary sense. Because the token, the *arrabon* of the promise, points toward the future, one has no capacity to repeat it in an act that turns out toward others. This would seem to put a promise closer to the pure and unilateral gift of Derrida, since for him the gift never arrives and never ap-

17. Milbank, "Can a Gift Be Given?" p. 129.
18. The communication of the promise itself will concern us in Chapter 5, below.
19. This important point is made by Oswald Bayer and John Milbank. See Oswald Bayer, "Ethik der Gabe," in *Die Gabe: Ein "Urwort" der Theologie?* ed. Veronika Hoffmann (Frankfurt: Verlag Otto Lembeck, 2009), pp. 115-66; John Milbank, *Being Reconciled: Ontology and Pardon* (London: Routledge, 2003), p. 147.

pears so it can never be mastered. Rather, as Stephen Webb points out, the gift is endlessly disseminated with abandon. It cannot be intentionally given without suffering the demands and force of exchange.[20] Milbank preserves this aspect of the pure gift in his emphasis on the aleatoric character of the repeated gift.

Thus, a promise, if it is going to enable giving, must do so in a surprising fashion but also in a way that promotes an appropriate giving that arises from but does not continue the promise. It may appear alien to the given situation but it is so only in order to stop or expose its distortion and to seek out more fitting and beneficial gifts.

4.3. Promise as Interruption

If a gift does not interrupt or in some way challenge the given, the gift does not afford any critical resources over and against the demands facing its recipients. Grace may fulfill or perfect nature but it does not do so without radically transforming it. To claim that gifts leave what they come to unchanged, or ignore the experiences and life that is already carrying on, is to risk that the gift merely continues what already is the case, fails to introduce new imperatives or new initiatives, and more or less certifies reality as it currently presents itself. The gift must do something with what is merely or already given, the manifold regions, spheres, cycles, and worlds. What we call the given is our situation, our experience, our history — in short, all the forces, demands, and things that appear to us. The given is our world as it appears to us. What is given to us is of course not reducible to the gift of creation since that would baptize the given, the current state of affairs that we experience, as God's intentions for the world. We cannot succumb to the temptation to naturalize our experiences as simply the essential character of our lives. We run the risk of sculpting into permanence all the inequities, injuries, and distortions that prop up or result from our state of affairs. Thus the given is an impure and impossibly complex mixture of creation, distorted creation, ambiguity, and uncertainty. It must address a need or stop a destructive act. Promise indeed addresses the given but it does so first to interrupt and then to recognize the other.[21]

Of course, the archaic or exchanged gift can interrupt as well. One can simply refuse to return, to reject the exchange, to stop and suffer the conse-

---

20. Webb, *The Gifting God*, pp. 154-57.

21. What I call interruption can stand in for a variety of critical practices, all of which can be summarized with Michel Foucault's slightly coy definition of criticism: "the art of not being governed so much." See Michel Foucault, "Qu'est-ce que la critique? [Critique et Aufklärung]," *Bulletein de la Société française de Philosophie* 84 (1990): 38.

quences. One can also challenge others by giving more than they do. Mauss accounts for all of these possibilities, the kinds of giving an archaic or reciprocated gift that respects the obligations and force of previous moments in the exchange. This is to deal with the given entirely out of whatever is available to one in one's state of affairs. Paul Ricoeur recommends this course when he claims that the archaic gift-cycle is not entirely and utterly pernicious, that not all force is negative and not all demands injury. Rather than seeking a gift or practice that can replace or undermine this cycle, Ricoeur advocates the use of critical discernment.[22] But since a promise is not reducible to the archaic or reciprocal gift, we can only consider how promise supports this kind of discrimination between beneficial and dangerous reciprocity.

Promise, in its first gift as a token, is a nothing and a something. It wavers, hanging in the air as a possibility or even as an incredulous offering. In this, promise comes close to the pure gift, and no gift is more interruptive than Derrida's pure gift. Indeed, he argues that it creates a cataclysm, or, in his terms, an event. More exactly, he holds that while a gift is impossible, "a gift could be possible, there could be a gift only at the instant an effraction in the circle will have taken place, at the instant all circulation will have been interrupted and on the condition of this instant."[23] The very whisper of a promise, the offering of its token, can disturb. As a gift that indeed does refer to the given, to the already existing motions and events in play, it arrives and implodes the given. As we saw in the case of the Hospitality of Sarah and Abraham, the mere mention of a child calls laughter from Sarah, if not total incredulity. The visitors promise the impossible. Their promise calls attention to the demands placed on the patriarchal couple, whether those demands are social or material. The promise of a child is both too much and too little. It is excessive, but also it could be so unbelievable as to be utterly nothing. To trust this promise is to dwell in it and to so share in its surprising and risky character. To trust the new is to become it, after a fashion. And so, the one who lives in promise becomes this kind of interruption, this kind of possibility that outstrips the given.

The other way that the pure gift induces trauma in the given is when it runs wild, jumps the rails of expectations, and refuses to answer any of the demands asked of it. Derrida calls this the dissemination of the gift without any return.[24] There is a sense that promise as a weak power also must go a little mad, as Derrida writes about the pure gift, because though a promise of-

---

22. Ricoeur, *Parcours de la reconnaissance,* pp. 369-77.

23. Jacques Derrida, *Given Time: 1. Counterfeit Money,* trans. Peggy Kamuf (Chicago: University of Chicago Press, 1992), p. 9.

24. Derrida, *Given Time,* p. 47.

fers a future, it does not secure it.[25] As we saw in our discussion of promise, power, and time, the weak power of God's promise does not hold out a future impervious to all contingencies. Rather, it is to commit to solidarity with Jesus, the forensic situation where the truth of Jesus and therefore the credibility of the promise is constantly under test. As we shall see, this weak power means that not only do the situations and claims that run counter to the promise contest its credibility, that God shall in fact fulfill it, but that God even contradicts it in God's own actions.

To dwell in the promise as interruption is to be witness to an event that occurs utterly by surprise, perhaps beyond all hope, which allows one to risk and most of all, to discover and shed light on the impurities of one's own life, the entanglements of one's own impure giving. To experience this interruption, to long for it, and to embody it in one's own person as dwelling in promise, is to set it alongside other situations and experiences, to call them into question, and indeed, to start to confront the failed gifts and strings that are offered by Christians to others. Interruption persists into recognition, even if we see that we cannot purely recognize the other through promise.

4.4. Misrecognition

Drawing from its critical moment, promise permits us to confront, participate in, and amend the many responsibilities, calls, demands, and aims that we confront in our existence even if we can only haltingly reach such accomplishments. This allows us to repent of and repair acts of misrecognition, and to freely give to the neighbor. This requires us to first consider recognition and the gift and then show how promise, though it is not repeated, enables recognition through a kind of impure giving.[26]

Gift-giving, alongside the moral dimensions of the material benefits transferred, offers recognition. Recognition is a moral act by which we are able to act and live with the other as they are. Failing to give, or giving in a way that diminishes another, is not just the aesthetic failure of failing to offer a proper present. Since gift-exchange is a public process, the pathologies of gift-exchange result in acts of misrecognition. Misrecognition denotes a variety of processes. For instance, misrecognition occurs when a person comes to

25. Derrida, *Given Time*, p. 35.
26. There are many other possible ways to develop the moral norms promise provides. Recognition is but one act it affords. One might consider the moral dimensions of praise, of credit, or of the act of belief. I develop recognition owing to the foregrounding of gift as the means by which to think of promise.

be only a recipient and never is empowered as a giver. This person becomes a client of a patron, molded into a subservient location. This person is therefore misrecognized because of the injury this dynamic engenders. In general, it marks the way that a person can ignore another, treat a person as an object incapable of response, an "it" rather than a "thou," or fail to attend to the other's differences, particularity, and self-representation.

Misrecognition goes beyond simple insult, social status, or loss of dignity. I do not merely misrecognize another when I succumb to prejudice. It does not simply mean that I have failed to discern you properly, as if I fail to possess the proper aesthetic judgment to appreciate the turn of shade in a painting. If I cannot come to some understanding of Mark Rothko's *Seagram Mural Sketch* (1959) or fail to perceive the complexities of a film like Andrei Tarkovsky's *Solaris* (1972), presumably those shades and colors are still somewhere in the painting or film for more sensitive viewers to discover. Yet if I fail to recognize you, I have done you injury and denied you the respect and autonomy you are owed.

Rather than starting from an ideal version of recognition where we "will be seen even as we are seen," the task of recognition starts with injury. This does not mean that this negative moment, starting with pain or suffering makes those moments a kind of dialectical necessity where injury persists even in eternity, that the pain that we endure and suffer becomes a kind of infinite pain. Injury gives us a starting point to develop recognition as a moral act so that we can, first, establish the purpose of recognition as a way of alleviating or reconciling situations, institutions, and events of suffering; and, second, indicate the difficulties of pure moral action under the aegis of promise.

Misrecognition means that there is a failing in my approach to the other — in my self-understanding as well as my stance towards you. Misrecognition calls for a reevaluation of oneself as well as the other because it pertains not merely to oneself or the other. It also demands attention to the relationship that in some way mutually determines both oneself and another. Positively, Axel Honneth summarizes recognition in this way:

> To recognize someone is to perceive in his or her person a value quality that motivates us intrinsically to no longer behave egocentrically, but rather in accordance with the intentions, desires, and needs of that person. This makes clear that recognitional behavior must represent a moral act, because it lets itself be determined by the value of other persons.[27]

27. Axel Honneth, "Recognition as Ideology," in *Recognition and Power: Axel Honneth and the Tradition of Critical Social Theory,* ed. Bert van den Brink and David Owen (Cambridge: Cambridge University Press, 2007), p. 337.

This definition of recognition seems to reduce its moral significance to the social relationships apart from the material needs. While recognition has caused much wariness when it seems to refer only to a social good and not to the material requirements, rights, and conditions of human life, it has a wider and more nimble reference to that complex set of needs and conditions for human life.

Recognition arises from analysis of the social character of human beings, an analysis that provides much of the normative direction for recognition but also highlights its shortcomings. Axel Honneth and others have provided ground for the processes of recognition and given force to its moral norms in the psychological development of human beings. This shows that humans not only benefit but need recognition to thrive as social and political beings. Similarly, recognition can be overburdened as a moral act since it depends upon the norms that enable recognition just as much as the act itself. When described as a goal of moral action, recognition can privilege some forms of recognizing over others and is perhaps not nimble enough to encompass the astonishing diversity of life. Indeed, to seek recognition can itself be pathological if the recognition sought reinforces destructive social roles or situations of material disadvantage.

Recognition only operates morally when it occurs mutually and is of common beneficence.[28] Since gift-exchange is a public act whereby partners mutually recognize each other, each kind of gift that scholars have advocated involves recognition in vastly different ways. The principal thrust of many forms of the unilateral, unconditional, or pure gifts occurs under the requirements of anonymity, giving at a distance, or utter unknowing. The giver and gift do not know each other in a way that permits a mutual recognition between giver and recipient.[29] As Ricoeur has shown, the exchange of gifts can be taken as an act of recognition between the parties. Thus, promise is an act by which God recognizes those upon whom God has rested God's Spirit, join-

---

28. See Axel Honneth, *The Struggle for Recognition: The Moral Grammar of Social Conflicts,* trans. Joel Anderson (Cambridge: MIT Press, 1995), pp. 92-130; Ricoeur, *Parcours de la reconnaissance,* pp. 317-40.

29. Kathryn Tanner's model does not afford mutual recognition. See Tanner, *Economy of Grace,* pp. 63-64. Though she makes use of a philosophical ethicist's discussion of gratitude in gift-giving to show how continuing to give is a free and autonomous act on the part of the human being, she excises mutual recognition. For gratitude to inject freedom in the exchange of gifts the gift-giving has to be beneficial in a way mutually understood by both parties. Since Tanner takes giving to occur without a name and so absent a giver, her model cannot use gratitude in this way. For Tanner, recognition may occur only in one direction: from the giver to the recipient.

ing them to the body of God's Son. And, likewise, to explore the subjectivity or personhood of the one promised, one would need to consider the trust offered to God to be an act of counter-recognition. But since we do not consider the effect of promise to be an act by which one goes on to give to others, and to so recognize others, the gift of promise does not immediately continue in its dispersal. This prevents the promise itself from being the direct means by which one recognizes the neighbor. Rather, the promise creates, by giving an other-directed possibility, a moral *sensorium*, that is, a capacity and sensitivity. Promise introduces an impulse for imagination and engenders a way of approaching the world that allows for recognizing the other.

This sensorium permits attention to the ways that we participate in impure giving, and indeed valorizes that giving. We should not expect too much from our attention to gifts; we cannot describe them as pure when they are mixed with failure and therefore impure. We cannot hope for too much to come from our efforts to recognize our neighbors and ourselves. They will always escape us as strangers; we will clumsily flatten their differences and erase some of their distinctiveness. We cannot see ourselves immediately and repair our distortions and our implications in forms of strong power. What we can do is to embrace others and enter into solidarity with them while repenting and repairing our own tattered histories. Promise enables us to give of ourselves. It does not enable us to give of ourselves purely and without failing. It allows us to confront and interrupt chains of giving that force and deprive others. But it does not absolve us of the need to implicate ourselves in those distortions. Promise cannot baptize all events as events of grace. But it can aid us in anticipating them and welcoming them when they arrive. Most of all, it can permit the kind of public and careful discernment of when to give and when to leave alone, when to engage, and when to repent. Promise is other-directed possibility and so this is never a power that forces itself on another but is nimble enough to resist the temptation to give. While archaic gifts demand a continuance of the circle, promise allows gifts to remain, to be taken up, or to be stopped. Since promise offers this possibility, it allows for the public discussion of whether this or that gift is beneficial since it allows for other ways of being than those that are at hand. It permits this kind of critical discussion because it does not endorse any given but allows us to obtain some distance from the given in the possible and allows us to imagine, plan, and otherwise discern what may be needful. Promise therefore creates a double place, as Luther wrote: dwelling in the neighbor and in Christ's body, which we call the church.

4.5. The Contradiction of Promise

Much speaks against the credibility of God's promise: the failures of life, the impotence of the good, and the fragility of reconciliation. The expectation of the promise's fulfillment allows us to test out its credibility, to consider how it might be if the world will be as God promises it to be, to consider how justice would be done if God accomplishes it in the eschaton of the promise, and to measure the distance that obtains between our fragmentary accomplishments and that fulfillment. Indeed, the impure giving to which we are party itself awaits fulfillment and perfection. Since all gifts in the archaic sense fluctuate between being benefits and disastrous poison, the arrival of a gift is ambiguous, and its reception and return determine its ultimate character, Derrida has likewise pointed out that until the promise finally arrives, one cannot perceive the difference between a promise and a threat.[30]

In order to consider this situation and to honor the risk, extension, and doubling that constitutes promise, promise must be public and publicly tested. But these ordinary disputations about the credibility of the promise and its distinction from a threat pale in comparison to an even more serious rejection of the promise: God may turn out to be the most significant burr in God's own promise. No text shows this better than the Binding of Isaac (Gen. 22:1-19). Abraham's strange act of obedience to offer Isaac on Moriah has fueled many reflections on the intersection of moral action, divinity, and the other. Here the trial occurs by God asking Abraham to sacrifice Isaac. God's command opposes God's promise. Gerhard von Rad's interpretation of this text sets it as summarizing the experience of Israel with God: this God is dangerous and demands Israel to hold to God despite all else, including God.[31] This truly is a trial, as the first verse of the Binding of Isaac states.

This touches on significant questions about the unity of God's actions and, in that unity, the cohesion of God. It seems that to assert that this text is an instance of God against God, as von Rad does, would fracture God's very being and unity, introduce turmoil into God's eternal life, and render God unworthy of love and trust. It would seem that such a contradiction of God by God would entail a darker or hidden God that lies behind the Triune God revealed in Jesus. But if we stick to the promise and its phenomenology, we can be sure to see that a promise without risk and contradiction is not worthy of

30. Jacques Derrida, "Réponses de Jacques Derrida," in *La Philosophie au risqué de la promesse,* ed. Marc Crépon and Marc de Launay (Paris: Bayard, 2004), pp. 197-98.
31. Gerhard von Rad, *Das Opfer des Abrahams* (Munich: Chr. Kaiser Verlag, 1971), pp. 34-37.

the name. Von Rad points out that to assert that God disturbs promise and actively works against it is to validate the very experience of life with the God of Israel. It is not to resolve this conflict ahead of time by either folding all of God's acts unmistakably into the Triune God nor is it to resolve the matter prematurely in favor of a more dualistic conception of God.

We do not need to go so far in either direction. To live in promise is to recognize this situation of lack and wealth. It is to honor what Luther called "the light of glory," that the resolution and establishment of God as a God of promise is finally a matter for God though we may dispute and debate its truth.[32] Promise itself bars the speculative resolution of this contradiction. Not that it means that God is graceful in entirety, immanently as well as economically, but that promise refuses to reconcile or eliminate experiences of God that contradict the promise. To do so would mean it was a clear window to reality instead of a hope and a possibility. To assert this identity would eliminate the promise and its risk. This giving over into the public consideration, this eschatological deferral, occurs in a place, indeed, it gives place, so it is to the topology of promise that we now turn.

32. Martin Luther, "Bondage of the Will (1525)," in *Luther and Erasmus: Free Will and Salvation,* ed. E. Gordon Rupp and Philip S. Watson, trans. E. Gordon Rupp et al. (Philadelphia: Westminster Press, 1969), p. 332. On the "light of glory," see Thomas Reinhuber, *Kämpfender Glaube: Studien zu Luthers Bekenntnis am Ende von* De servo arbitrio (Berlin: Walter de Gruyter, 2000), pp. 186-94, 226-34.

CHAPTER 5

The Topology of Promise

D'un gent entre chien et la loup.

Johann Georg Hamann,
"Letztes Blatt," 1788

A promise, like any gift, occurs someplace and goes somewhere. Gifts attend to and depend upon place just as much as the agents who give and receive them: their origins and destinations matter to their exchange. To put it differently, gifts give place by their exchange and where they are refused. This idiom, "to give place," brings us to the final interval of our inquiry, since giving or taking place refers to more than just the appearance of an object within or at coordinates of location in abstract space. To give or take place, which is expressed by *topos*, means to hold body, to engage physical surroundings, those webs of intricate relationships that make up a locale, and to enable the formation and action of a community. This place can also be considered the sacrament of the promise. This place is the Eucharist. And this Eucharist adjoins promise's other place: the neighbor.

To ask after place is to put the question of being to promise in another way, as well as to inquire after the interpretive practices that it affords. Such a consideration of place is to develop what Heidegger calls a "topology of Being."[1] Still, while promise gives place far differently than Heidegger understood

1. Martin Heidegger, "Seminar in Le Thor, 1969," in *Gesamtausgabe*, vol. 15: *Seminare*, ed. Curd Ochwadt (Frankfurt: Klostermann Verlag, 1986), p. 344. Jeffrey Malpas has provided an exhaustive and genetic-developmental account of Heidegger's writings as primarily concerning place. See Malpas, *Heidegger's Topology: Being, Place, World* (Cambridge: MIT Press, 2006).

his gift to give a place to dwell, the efforts he undertook to recover place from its obscurity, and to liberate it from the dominance of space as physical extension, provides an important starting point. For Heidegger, place is created by the exchange of gifts by those elements of existence that constitute a world. Place after Heidegger does not merely mark boundaries of community, but also gives an orientation on a map; indeed it gives the whole *mappa mundi*, the map of the globe. Therefore, to think about place allows us to consider how promise and world interact, or the liturgical dimensions of the promise. Inquiring after the place of promise will allow us to further follow the reorientation of ourselves in promise, to replace the question "Who are you?" with "Where are you?"[2]

Further, attention to place allows us to consider God's actions in a concrete and localized fashion. Our stress on the Lord's Supper as the *topos* of promise parallels the connection between justification by faith alone and baptism made by the *Joint Declaration on the Doctrine of Justification*.[3] By showing that justification occurs somewhere, and that this place is baptism, a significant dimension of Luther's practice and theology of baptism takes on ecumenical significance. To consider the place of promise likewise shows the post-foundational character of promise as a doubled and extended gift, making it available to consider as a practice and as encompassing a community.

Since God's promise in the Crucified One enables other forms of giving and receiving, hosting and being guests, this chapter concludes our analysis of promise as gift through a consideration of the communication of promise itself, the giving and offering of promise. Unlike the kinds of gift we have considered and the places they give, promise occurs in a place and opens up to other places. Promise occurs in the Lord's Supper, which is Jesus' offering of himself to eat and drink in the midst of communal betrayal. The Eucharist gathers and scatters. These motions have been expressed in the prayer associated with the Supper as described in the Didache: "As this broken bread was scattered upon the mountaintops and after being harvested was made one, so let your church be gathered together from the ends of the earth into your kingdom."[4] But this

2. Jean-Yves Lacoste, *Expérience et absolu: Questions disputées sur l'humanité de l'homme* (Paris: Presses Universitaires de France, 1994), p. 7.

3. International Lutheran–Roman Catholic Dialogue, *Joint Declaration on the Doctrine of Justification* (1999), in *Growth in Agreement II: Reports and Agreed Statements of Ecumenical Conversations on a World Level, 1982-1998*, ed. Jeffrey Gros, Harding Meyer, and William G. Rusch (Grand Rapids: Eerdmans, 2000), p. 570. See Wolfhart Panennberg, "Die Rechtfertigungslehre im okumenischen Gesprach," in *Beitrage zur systematischen Theologie*, vol. 3 (Gottingen: Vandenhoeck & Ruprecht, 1999), p. 286.

4. Didache 9:4, in Kurt Niederwimmer, *The Didache: A Commentary*, ed. Harold W. Attridge, trans. Linda M. Maloney (Minneapolis: Fortress Press, 1998), p. 144.

gathering rejects as it welcomes; it disperses while inviting in. It gives place in the sense that it opens up the possibility of encounter and love but it also gives place in that it affords its participants a chance to resist efforts of domination, evisceration, and the distortion of economies. This place occurs since the Lord's Supper is the place where Jesus gives himself, a communication and anamnesis of his sacrifice that is promise. It is also a place where we may, dwelling in the Spirit, remind God of God's promise. The dynamics of the Lord's Supper, where the public character of promise takes hold since it is the anamnesis of Jesus' death, in which the Spirit, with those assembled, bids God to be faithful and to bring again the promise of the Crucified One. This is a public accounting of promise, of holding God to God's promise, as well as a repetition of God's making of the promise in the crucifixion and resurrection of Jesus. These are not events to be secreted away, revealed to a few. Nor are they utterly lost to the past. Rather, in the repetition of the promise, they give place; intersecting with other places, the Lord's Supper gives the place of the neighbor.

5.1. Inalienable Gifts and Place

Gift-exchange requires a discussion of place because gift-exchange creates shared place as well as difference by drawing boundaries. If all archaic giving creates relationships and therefore difference, those relationships and differences vary according to the kind of giving and receiving. For instance, if one receives from the other and never returns, this establishes a relationship of client and patron. Likewise, gender relationships can be maintained by the varying gifts and offerings exchanged. Most of all, to not give, to have a relationship of neither giving nor receiving, denotes the stranger and outsider. By creating relationships, the offering of gifts navigates both the place in which people dwell and the places across which they travel and communicate. For instance, Marcel Mauss describes instances of strangers meeting and concludes, "Two groups of men who meet can only either draw apart, and, if they show mistrust towards one another or issue a challenge, fight — or they can negotiate." To meet with the stranger is to always dwell in an "unstable state between festival [of exchange] and war."[5] Gift-exchange seems to always involve the establishment and destruction of boundaries.[6]

Boundaries are established because archaic gifts seek their home; in

---

5. Marcel Mauss, *The Gift: Form and Reason for Exchange in Archaic Societies,* trans. W. D. Halls (New York: Norton, 1990), p. 82.

6. Marshal Sahlins, *Stone Age Economics* (New York: Routledge, 2004), pp. 149-84.

fact, their circuit from and ultimate return to a homeland define them as archaic gifts. In Mauss's account, they seek their origin because of a certain inalienability; they cannot be ultimately made alien or other to that place. Though they wander, their spirit seeks to return to its origin. Annette Weiner replaces Mauss's quasi-theological account of gift-exchange with the idea of inalienable gifts. Rather than accepting his account of the *hau*, which attributes agency to the gifts themselves, she shows that gifts circulate in order to prevent other, more valuable gifts from being lost. Participants in gift-exchange try to dislodge these priceless items by offering gifts. Thus, for Weiner, the inalienable is what sets in motion the circle of exchange.[7] What is not given is precisely the most important of all. The keeping of these special items that cannot circulate all but defines "origin."[8] The boundary of a community is marked by those who do not participate or share in this inalienable gift. Promise offers community, yet it has borders that are porous because it is sustained by being a doubled and extended gift.

By contrast, the pure or unilateral gift does not seek its origin. In fact, it shuns it, disavowing its parentage in order to maintain its freedom. It stays quiet about itself so that it does not call attention to any obligation that it might bring. The pure gift may have something to do with its home as it obliquely interrupts ordinary and archaic gift-exchanges, but it is forevermore taking leave of any place. It is "atopic," as Jacques Derrida writes, and, just as with time, it interrupts and scatters.[9] Similarly, Kathryn Tanner's version of the unilateral gift employs the model of anonymous charitable giving that obscures the origin of a gift in order to sever any relationship between donor and recipient.[10] John Milbank, on the other hand, identifies the locale of his purified gift-exchange in the Eucharist itself, though the place of gift-exchange for him is properly the Triune God repeated differently in all other places.[11] Promise takes up elements of the atopic, and of location in God, but does so in a way that drives those promised toward the neighbor's locale, since it points forward to another locale — it does not seek to return to an or-

7. Annette B. Weiner, *Inalienable Possessions: The Paradox of Keeping-While-Giving* (Berkeley: University of California Press, 1992), pp. 152-55.

8. Some anthropologists go on to describe these inalienable and unmovable objects as the source of sacred space. See Maurice Godelier, *The Enigma of Gift,* trans. Nora Scott (Chicago: University of Chicago Press, 1999), pp. 177-98.

9. Jacques Derrida, *Given Time: 1. Counterfeit Money,* trans. Peggy Kamuf (Chicago: University of Chicago Press, 1992), p. 53.

10. Kathryn Tanner, *Economy of Grace* (Minneapolis: Fortress Press, 2005), pp. 47-85.

11. John Milbank, "Can a Gift Be Given? Prolegomena to a Future Trinitarian Metaphysic," *Modern Theology* 11 (1995): 154.

igin. It comes from somewhere, from the room in which Jesus declared his testament to the community of friends that would soon betray him. It offers another locale, a coming community of love and forgiveness. It forms a community waiting for community. To celebrate the Lord's Supper is to live in these two places, a place between that remembers and so makes present Jesus' betrayal and death, and also waits for his arrival. These exchanges and offerings make a place; they require it and etch it out even while they are marked by failure and rejection. Heidegger's recovery of place will organize our exploration of how the Lord's Supper is the quasi-transcendental condition of promise and its locale.

5.2. Place

Place refers to not only location or spatial extension but also to the conditions that enable embodiment, communication, and action. To inquire after what makes something a place is not merely to reduce something physical to its spatial dimensions but to bring space together with time as a way to consider the conditions of life's flourishing. The return to place in many academic studies and disciplines signals a way to conceptualize phenomena in an alternative way than in terms of abstract space.[12]

In topology, space refers to extension. In many ways, the construction of reality through the category of space, a process frequently identified as "spatialization," eliminates place through a process of homogenization. To consider location in space is to treat every phenomenon uniformly and to reduce each to fit the coordinates of pure space as a kind of atemporal physical extension. This kind of space is indifferent to locale, to regional variation, and to individuality. Historians of modernity describe spatialization as that process in which this notion of space comes to determine ordinary understandings of body, practice, and world.[13] Though this abstraction is necessary for

12. See Edward S. Carey, *The Fate of Place: A Philosophical History* (Berkeley: University of California Press, 1997); Luce Irigaray, *An Ethics of Sexual Difference*, trans. Carolyn Burke and Gillian C. Gill (Ithaca: Cornell University Press, 1993), pp. 34-55; Elizabeth Grosz, *Space, Time, and Perversion* (London: Routledge, 1995), pp. 111-24. Vitor Westhelle discusses a variety of other kinds of space as a resource for developing ecclesiology as event in *The Church Event: Call and Challenge of a Church Protestant* (Minneapolis: Fortress Press, 2010), pp. 137-53.

13. This, in broad strokes, is a common theme among the otherwise divergent evaluations of modernity in the following works: Richard Rorty, *Philosophy and the Mirror of Nature* (Oxford: Blackwell, 1980), pp. 32-70, 114-24; Jürgen Habermas, *Der philosophisches Diskurs der Moderne: Zwölf Vorlesungen* (Frankfurt: Suhrkamp, 1991), pp. 9-33; Stephen Toulmin: *Cos-

the practices of the natural sciences, where space operates as a pure "container" for reality, it does not reflect, nor does it relate to, the interaction of place with human and nonhuman beings. Further, when reproduced in human life, this abstract conceptuality of space constricts and limits human possibilities and generates pathological human social relations.[14] Finally, the predominance of space as abstracted extension supports "view from nowhere" epistemologies, accounts of knowing, acting, and being that disregard the particular standpoints from which humans make judgments.[15] Such a "view from nowhere" can engender a way of interpretation that ignores the role of the pre-understanding, the way that human beings are situated and how that contributes to the act of understanding.

Place allows us to consider how practices engage people and things in ways other than as objects. That is, it allows us to consider the way that gift and communities give rise to each other by virtue of what is given. To be sure, the use of place leads some to consider the true "objective" nature of reality to be fundamentally space in the sense of extension, and that place is merely the affective or subjective experience of extension. This upholds a strict and insuperable division between what is natural and what humans create, as in the binaries of the found and the made, the natural and the cultural. In contrast, Heidegger and his successors argue that place does not merely arise from the way that humans interpret the world but that there is a sense in which the world makes human beings. To consider place first and spatiality as physical extension second shows the reciprocal and interwoven character of the natural and the cultural. Jeffrey Malpas defines place as "the idea of an open yet bounded realm in which the things of the world can appear and within which events can 'take place.'"[16] He reproduces the idiom with which this chapter began, which would seem like a tautology — that place gives place. Yet in fact

---

mopolis: The Hidden Agenda of Modernity (Chicago: University of Chicago Press, 1990); Catherine Pickstock, After Writing: On the Liturgical Consummation of Philosophy (Oxford: Blackwell, 1998), pp. 47-100; Charles Taylor, A Secular Age (Cambridge: Belknap, 2007), pp. 159-211.

14. For example, as Luce Irigaray points out in her own efforts toward the recovery of place, to take space as a pure receptivity, a blank screen onto which time allows things to appear, is a way to perpetuate the association of women with receptivity and passivity by their being a "space." See Irigaray, Ethics of Sexual Difference, pp. 5-19.

15. There exists a strong affinity, as this paragraph shows, between our proposals and standpoint epistemology. For theological uses of standpoint epistemology, which has its genesis in feminist philosophy of science, see Graham Ward, Cultural Transformation and Religious Practice (Cambridge: Cambridge University Press, 2005), pp. 72-85.

16. Jeffery Malpas, Place and Experience: A Philosophical Topography (Cambridge: Cambridge University Press, 1999), p. 33.

this definition shows that a place gives *others* place: it assigns roles, possibilities, and sets space and time in motion. Place is both a condition of space and time and something that reproduces itself in and for others. To put it differently, Jean-Yves Lacoste defines place as that which "furnishes us the coordinates of life and existence."[17] But each place differs in its singularity and uniqueness; the place of one gift is wholly different from another. Promise creates place by giving the place of the neighbor.

5.3. Heidegger and Place

Promise gives place in the Eucharist. As a meal, a collection of elements and a movement by which Christ's death is proclaimed until he comes again (1 Cor. 11:26), it is no wonder that many writers have used the category of gift to discuss the Eucharist.[18] These contributions take many directions and starting points but here we shall consider Eucharist from the perspective of the Last Supper. In each of these cases, we shall consider how the Eucharist is neither purely a gathering nor is it entirely a dispersal. It does not quite qualify as a place in the sense given by Heidegger since, when the Eucharist is the place of promise, it resists the kind of collection that Heidegger believes a place accomplishes. It is not bounded to a particular locale in the same fashion as the dwelling he discovers in the places he uses as examples: the bridge, the house, the jug.[19]

Heidegger explicitly shows how place and gift are intimately related in some of his later writings, even though he utilizes a mythological concept he calls the "fourfold" to explain these relationships. He considers place to be "open" in that it creates a clearing for the gathering of others, but a place emerges from what he calls the play of the fourfold. This fourfold giving-and-receiving of earth, sky, mortals, and gods gives place for the late Heidegger. When he considers particular things that give place, he considers them in terms of how this thing — such as a jug — gives an offering to the gods and to mortals, how it receives water from the sky and the earth. In his view, the jug gathers together the entire elements of the world.

The world constituted by Heidegger's fourfold is another world than

17. Lacoste, *Expérience et absolu,* p. 8.
18. See David N. Power, *Sacrament: The Language of God's Giving* (New York: Herder & Herder, 1999), pp. 274-310.
19. Martin Heidegger, "Building, Dwelling, Thinking" and "The Thing," in *Poetry, Language, and Thought,* trans. Albert Hofstadter (New York: Harper & Row, 1971), pp. 143-62, 163-86.

that of the God of Israel and the atmosphere of the New Testament writings, since the Heideggerian world owes itself to a German-Greco amalgamation.[20] If we tried to inquire how the Lord's Supper is a thing and therefore a place in Heidegger's sense, we would be inscribing it in a narrative alien to it. For instance, in the Eucharist, Jesus receives betrayal and desertion while offering those gathered his very body and blood. This would short-circuit Heidegger's fourfold since it would have the gods dying and mortals severing and betraying the gods, offerings and exchanges that Heidegger's scheme cannot tolerate. In light of this difficulty, though it would be easy to dismiss these four dimensions of the world as a bald return to myth and poetry, a close reading of Heidegger's development of the fourfold shows that earth and sky are spatial dimensions of the world and gods and mortals represent the origin and destiny of time.[21] When one arranges these four elements on horizontal and vertical axes, they function as the interaction of the temporal exchange of goal and origin, ground and limit. This interpretation can overcome the esotericism of Heidegger's fourfold in order to consider the thing and place's act to give, receive, and let be.[22]

For Heidegger, the thing gives place by being an event of gift-exchange along the lines expressed in Weiner's anthropological research.[23] Each thing gathers, receives, and offers the fourfold. Whether it is to receive or to give, to recognize or to let be, Heidegger considers his examples as things in terms of their ability to pour out, as in the case of the jug, and so to give to the divinities or to mortals. A bridge gathers by uniting the sky and earth and affording mortals a way to traverse. These dimensions of gift-exchange are summarized in Heidegger's constant repetition throughout these late writings that the thing gathers, offers, stays, and marks limits. Indeed this, he notes, is the older

20. See John D. Caputo, *Demythologizing Heidegger* (Bloomington: Indiana University Press, 1993), pp. 169-85.

21. Malpas, *Heidegger's Topology*, p. 256.

22. I follow John Milbank's analysis of the essay "The Thing" in John Milbank, "The Thing Given," *Archivio di filosofia* 74 (2006): 503-39. Milbank does not discuss place. Emmanuel Levinas stands in for many when he criticizes Heidegger's fourfold as a return to paganism with its fetishization of sacred groves. See Levinas, "Heidegger, Gagarin, and Us," in *Difficult Freedom: Essays on Judaism*, trans. Séan Hand (Baltimore: Johns Hopkins University Press, 1990), pp. 231-34. Heidegger's attention to place has often been tied to his discussion of "homeland," as well as to his involvement in National Socialism. For a discussion of this and many other issues related to Heidegger's politics, see Jeff Malpas, "Geography, Biology, and Politics," in *Heidegger and the Thinking of Place: Explorations in the Topology of Being* (Cambridge: MIT Press, 2011), pp. 137-58.

23. This is especially the case in "Zeit und Sein," in Martin Heidegger, *Zur Sache des Denkens* (Tübingen: Max Niemeyer, 1969), pp. 8-9.

meaning of the thing, such as when assemblies or gatherings in public were called a thing.[24] Place, we may surmise from Heidegger's analysis, is itself sustained by the circular exchange of forces and elements distinguished by their spatial or temporal directionality.

But most of all, for Heidegger, place emerges from a world. *World* for him denotes the horizon of being and existence that is established by how a thing gives a boundary:

> A space is something that has been made room for, something that is cleared and free, namely within a boundary, Greek *peras*. A boundary is not that at which something stops but, as the Greeks recognized, the boundary is that from which something begins its presencing.[25]

The boundary created by giving and receiving that marks where origin begins and ends creates a boundary, and so space for beings to emerge, which corresponds to the way that the inalienable gift allows for difference and social structures to emerge. It is this boundary, which sometimes is called a horizon or limit, that makes for a space generated by a place. In the absence of a boundary that clearly marks off a space, Heidegger finds confusion and disorder since people, natural objects, and things made by humans would no longer have a proper home. They would wander, homeless, apart from their origin. Heidegger's view gives considerable aid to the understanding of gift and boundary developed by Weiner and her successors, since her analysis did not expressly bring place to the foreground.

But Heidegger goes even further by pointing out how gift-exchange gives rise to a world by making space. Out of his analysis Heidegger claims that the thing gives space (and time) by being this place of gift-exchange. Having considered promise and time, the weak promise that is God's also plays a role in establishing place differently than other kinds of gift. Heidegger takes space to be physical extension and calls it a "clearing" where events may occur by virtue of the limits and boundaries created by gift-exchange. In an exacting but compressed paragraph from his "Art and Space," Heidegger outlines place and its relationship to home or origin:

> Still, how can we find the unique characteristics of space? We shall seek to listen to the language. From where does it speak the word 'space'? It speaks therein of clearing. This means, to clear out, to make free from the wilderness. Clearing-away brings the free, the open for the living and set-

24. Heidegger, "The Thing," p. 177.
25. Heidegger, "Building, Dwelling, Thinking," p. 154.

tling of human beings. Clearing, when thought in its characteristics, is a freeing-up of places in which the destiny of the dwelling human being turns to the wholeness of a home or the brokenness of homelessness or in ambivalence toward each.[26]

Heidegger considers place to be an event that gives space and time as well as something that gathers together a variety of elements that make up the world by tying them to their origin and making them to be at home by putting them on to their proper destiny. Similarly, it corresponds to the relationship between place and gift in the archaic or reciprocated gift, since in that kind of gift-exchange the gift's progress always occurs in a circle, returning toward its origin and so defining home and homelessness by the boundaries of its recipients and donors. Place is here defined by its reception and in terms of offering. As he writes, "We must learn to think that the things themselves are place and do not only belong to a place."[27] We could summarize his work on place along these lines: a place joins community and marks boundaries by its reception and giving. It shows how existence can be lived in a place and emerges from the interplay of gift, even if we demur that the fourfold that Heidegger proposes enables such life.

Place can also imply non-place by the borders it draws. What lies beyond is the wild, that which has not been cleared for human dwelling. But there is yet another beyond both of these. Lacoste has engaged this definition of place in order to show how liturgy offers a way to transcend it completely. While Lacoste shows the worry that place denotes a total and complete determination of being, an exhaustion of what is possible given a particular place, he notes that liturgy subverts place in Heidegger's sense. He aims to subvert the topological "in terms of eschatological anticipation."[28] Lacoste holds that place must be supplanted by non-place, that the place given in the world is transgressed through liturgy. By expecting more than this world, this space that is marked off by the boundaries of gift-exchange, the world is both transfigured and exceeded. Catherine Pickstock, likewise, opposes Heidegger's view of place to one that is ultimately "located in God."[29] Both Pickstock and Lacoste offer this transcendent place (or non-place, as Lacoste calls it) as an alternative to an entirely immanent and this-worldly understanding of place.

---

26. Martin Heidegger, "Kunst und Raum," in *Aus der Erfahrung des Denkens,* vol. 13 of *Gesamtausgabe,* ed. Hermann Heidegger (Frankfurt: Klostermann, 1983), p. 206.

27. Heidegger, "Kunst und Raum," p. 208.

28. Lacoste, *Expérience et absolu,* pp. 28-29.

29. Pickstock, *After Writing,* p. 232.

Pickstock holds that it is precisely the location that God is in Godself that displaces the ordinary limitations of place:

> [God] occupies space even before there is a space, and occupies it more than it occupies itself. God is also preoccupied in relation to space because He is displaced: He is permanently concerned with the Other. In Himself he is ecstatically preoccupied.[30]

Pickstock holds that the infinity of God precludes the location of God in an ordinary or immanent sense but that this infinity and the human participation in God through the Eucharist allow humans to transcend the limitations of place. To put it differently, Heidegger's view of place does not ever allow for one dwelling in a place to exceed the possibilities that each place gives; the ways that the fourfold interact are determined by the thing that variously gives and takes from them. Since promise offers possibility to the other, Lacoste and Pickstock point us in a proper direction beyond Heidegger's determination of place. Though place signals the concrete and determinate locations that all things and people hold, if they are as Heidegger describes them, they are only given to the immanent possibilities available in the circumscribed place and not by the possibility given by the Spirit. Thus, like Lacoste, we seek the Eucharist as place and as non-place, a dis-place-ment of all local rootedness that moves toward another home. Unlike Lacoste and Pickstock, however, we must consider how the Eucharist is porous to the other's place.

Thus, Lacoste and Pickstock offer the eternal God as our destination. Though proper in one sense, this eternal and divine place for the gift offers a different orientation. This divine home that is naked of Christ deep in the flesh exceeds rather than embraces the neighbor's place. As doubled and extended gift, promise has its origin in the uneasy place of the Lord's Supper and looks forward to a place of community. Between these two, the place sought by promise is nowhere except the neighbor.

5.4. Eucharist

The place given in the Eucharist is a place marked by betrayal as much as by the offering of promise. No matter what liturgically frames the *Verba*, its first words always begin a new stage in the action of the Eucharist: "In the night in which he was betrayed." The Supper as place is comprised of the following

---

30. Pickstock, *After Writing,* p. 229.

features: the borrowed room, the ambiguous character of Jesus as host, and the promise that lies at the center of the cup and wine. These features each represent a particular dynamic of gift-exchange that engenders the promise. To repeat the promise, or to communicate it, is to remember this place as well as to step toward the neighbor. The gifts given and received in the Lord's Supper, and the very economy that it repeats again, are impure. It lacks purity because it is given and rejected by the community of Jesus' friends. The promise is indeed without strings; it does not demand. Jesus assumes all the demand of the promise himself. But the impurity of the promise is that it is made by Jesus who is betrayed. To pretend that this mark does not perpetually attend the promise is to sever it from this Jesus and his death and resurrection. But this rejection does not mean that the promise is only negative and a sign of disaster. It is both joy and sorrow. It is the medicine *(pharmakon)* of immortality and of mortal danger.

I will proceed to develop this place through a kind of commentary on the Eucharist, traversing through several common theological questions about the Eucharist. Each of these short stages in framing and unframing this place draws from both our discussion of Heidegger and from the definition of place that springs from the idea of the inalienable gift. This means that we do not valorize any particular liturgical order, even ones that lack the *Verba,* but attend to the biblical narratives and the traditions of the Eucharist in an ecumenical fashion. We shall take these up with a view to how promise as gift creates place and how it offers a limit out of which things might appear. The biblical narratives that discuss the Last Supper, that which is repeated in the *Verba,* always begin at nighttime, at the time of betrayal. This betrayal extends throughout the promise that the Supper offers and is not remedied or eliminated by any of the communities to which the Supper gives place. To be faithful to this betrayal is to celebrate this Supper in a way that communicates its promise and does so in a dis-possessive way, to mark that the promise alone sustains the friendships, the community, and the work done by what we call church.

This betrayal notes the dangerous character of the meal. To enter into its place is to risk betraying the one who offers his very self. Likewise, to presume to offer it on Christ's behalf is to assume the place of host. To put the *Verba* in another form: there is no host who is not betrayed, no community that it gathers that does not itself desert Jesus, and no exchange or action taken that is pure. The Lord's Supper is the place where promise is offered and therefore the feast in which one dwells, where one eats and drinks the very body and blood of Jesus to discover the possibility that the Spirit brings, an orientation to the other place of promise: the neighbor. And so, while we do not repeat the fixtures or architecture of this meal in its historical situation, we do repeat its place, the cup and paten that bear the bread and wine that we share. The repetition of this place comes about by the declaration of the promise, the prayer for the Spirit for the anamnesis of Jesus' sacrifice, and the longing for the fulfillment of the promise.

God mandates this repetition, to use classical language, tying it to promise.[31] Setting aside the complex historical and theological discussion of the discontinuities between the church's Supper and the one Jesus celebrated, we may state the following: the Triune God gives the Eucharist, remembering and making present this first meal together with Jesus' crucifixion and resurrection. This upper room, this place of betrayal, is repeated differently in the Spirit as the paten and cup are offered in the anamnesis of Jesus' self-giving. This is how these things gather together the place that is Eucharist. Each successive meal is gracious by the power of the Spirit, its other-directed possibility, joining those who eat and drink to the promise of God in the Crucified One. This meal is promise and so may be evaluated and debated to see if it is really beneficial. What the Spirit gives in representing Christ broken on his cross may be considered a promise and not a threat both in what it offers now, what place it opens up, and what it awaits in the eschaton.[32] We shall consider this place of promise in its dimensions.

To begin, it is Jesus who presides over this meal and place. Any host governs a place.[33] The host welcomes and rejects guests; the host oversees the domestication of strangers. The host functions as a patron to guests, who are the

31. "We call sacraments those rites, which have the mandate of God and to which are added the promise of grace." *Apology of the Augsburg Confession*, XIII, 3, in *The Book of Concord: The Confesssions of the Evangelical Lutheran Church*, ed. Robert Kolb and Timothy J. Wengert, trans. Charles Arand et al. (Minneapolis: Fortress Press, 2000), p. 219. This claim is ecumenical. See Group des Dombes, "L'Esprit Saint, L'Eglise et les Sacrements," in *Pour la communion des Eglises: L'apport du Groupe des Dombes (1937-1987)*, ed. Alain Blancy and Maurice Jourjon (Paris: Editions du Centurion, 1988), p. 117.

32. This sense of the institution of the sacraments by the Spirit is more fully articulated in Robert W. Jenson, *Systematic Theology*, vol. 2 (Oxford: Oxford University Press, 2000), pp. 178-88. Though Jenson more directly discusses institution by the Spirit and by Jesus, the discussion parallels that of individual sacraments or the sacramental matrix of the church itself. Jenson's position is confirmed by the framework given in Paul F. Bradshaw, *The Search for the Origins of Christian Worship: Sources and Methods for the Study of Early Liturgy*, 2nd ed. (Oxford: Oxford University Press, 2002), pp. 1-20, 47-71.

33. For a discussion of host and the power and duties in both Judaism and the Greco-Roman world, see Dennis E. Smith, *From Symposium to Eucharist: The Banquet in the Early Christian World* (Minneapolis: Fortress Press, 2003). Jacques Derrida discusses the host-guest relationship in "Une Hospitalité à L'Infini," in *Manifeste pour l'Hospitalité*, ed. Michel Wieviorka and Mohammed Seffahi (Grigny: Paroles D'Aube, 1999), pp. 97-106.

host's clients. It would be simple to establish Jesus as host along with those who act in Jesus' stead in celebrations of the Eucharist. Yet this place circumvents the ordinary dynamics of host and guest by the elision of the host. There can be no Eucharistic hospitality in this strong sense, in the sense that the host domesticates the outsiders, bringing them into the fold through the ministrations of the meal. There can be no host in this strong sense since God makes the promise by the death and resurrection of Jesus and the descent of the Spirit at Pentecost, a power that is weak and does not rule as the host does, excluding some possibilities and bringing others to actuality.

Jesus is a strange host in the borrowed upper room. Though he blesses the bread and wine and offers his promise, he does so in the anticipation of danger, if not death.[34] This is a moment of utter weakness and does not offer a promise that will preserve this moment in the face of the future. Jesus as host is weak like his promise and so is not merely the equal of his guests but is indebted to them by making this promise. He is obliged to fulfill it, to make good on his pledge. He opens himself up to their trust and skepticism alike, their anxiety and their fear. This event of promise is one of anticipation, pledged by his body and blood as bread and wine. Because he does not reserve anything, does not leave any gift behind, does not keep anything inalienable, there is no ultimate origin for the Supper. The place of promise is utterly placeless in the sense that the goods of the promise, its gifts, are utterly dispersed and handed over. This lack of inalienable gifts, things kept, means that there is no place to mark here and there in it; the host has divested himself of whatever status as host that he might have held.

The place of promise is and is not a place; it is in between the two. Heidegger's view of place is that there is a reservation, an inalienable gift at the heart of a place that marks it off; the host keeps something back from exchange, reserving it from exchange, preventing it from going around and being taken up by others. In his divestment, Jesus renders the Supper atopic. There is a tear and a rending of the fabric of the ordinary place for the sake of the neighbor. In this, the upper room is the place of promise and so is repeatable and utterly singular. It therefore is open to the possibility of the other.

Acting after Jesus, continuing on his place, the obligation of the community, those charged to declare it, is to simply communicate it to others. These peoples and communities do not host since they do not own or master the promise. There are no guests since there are no hosts. A host can discern

---

34. On this, see Ferdinand Hahn, "Zum Stand der Erforschung des urchristlichen Herrenmahls," *Evangelische Theologie* 35 (1975): 553-63.

who belongs to the community and who does not. But the promise rules out any sense that its location can be dominated or ruled by those charged to declare it. This does not mean that the churches have not and will not have tried to do so, domesticating this meal and making it their own feast instead of one that is itinerant, iterable, and open. The promise and this place opened up by a weak host can only be safeguarded by seeing to the repetition of the promise, its declaration, and following its mandate.

The aleatoric character of the Supper emerges from its location in a borrowed room.[35] Every event of the Lord's Supper occurs in a borrowed room even if it is celebrated in a centuries-old building or on a street corner. It so occurs since promise displaces the place in which it occurs, borrowing that place for the moment to declare betrayal and a future reconciliation. Thus, the place of promise is not fixed, whether one expects it to occur in a sacred site or to be kept out of the public or secular sphere. This means that like the unilateral or pure gift, promise is atopic: it cannot create a place nor sustain itself. Since promise occurs in the repetition of this place in the Spirit, we may find it anywhere and might discover the promise of the Crucified One declared, perhaps in surprising and unexpected locations.

And with these two layers of framing we come to the beginning of the *Verba:* "In the night in which he was betrayed." Every place where the promise is recalled and communicated can be neither fixed nor secured from all disaster. The promise of the Supper creates a community that is shattered and broken as well as rejected and dispelled. Since the Lord's Supper creates a place, this place is not one that has fixed boundaries as Heidegger articulates — it does not form a world in its entirety; instead, it opens itself up to other worlds by giving place to another. The pledge of bread and wine is a thing that gathers only to send and it offers only something else than the place where it dwells even as it gives Christ in advance. It does not draw a limit to mark itself off from other worlds, nor does it enclose a totality within itself. The Supper, in its promissory dis-possession, is porous to other places and non-places alike.

This means that it is both the nexus for a community of communities and a way toward the place of neighbor. Because this Supper shares itself and the place is multiple, repeated variously throughout the world and through history, this place remains shared as it creates communities both diachronically and synchronically. Each community is held together by recognizing itself in

---

35. On this setting and its role in the early theologies of the Eucharist, see Bruce Chilton, *A Feast of Meanings: Eucharistic Theologies from Jesus through Johannine Circles* (Leiden: Brill, 1994), pp. 63-74, 146-49.

and with others in the promise. "We receive one another with Christ and Christ with one another; we at once receive Christ and the church in which we receive him. That is, at Eucharist, we are precisely 'coembodiments' of Christ."[36] But this is not at the expense of the atopic character of the Eucharist. Instead, the promise can be present in any place and so disrupt that place. The Supper wanders, to be sure, but because the promise extends, it extends out in a diachronic community. It is not punctilinear, given to appearance only when the Supper is celebrated, withdrawn or nonexistent in the meanwhile. If that were the case, the promise would be completely reduced to a pure gift, obliquely related to the world and its history. It would be an event, to be sure, but it would not be the event that opens up in its extension as a promise does. It would require much more reflection on this continuity of the community and its attendant questions of institution, or its organs of continuity, such as apostolic succession, creed, or canon. Instead, we can apply the extension of promise into the communion ecclesiology well-summarized in ecumenical dialogue: "The one universal church is a communion of many communities and the local church a communion of persons."[37] The promise creates and requires a community, and it does in fact gather in and send out people in their various places since that promise's place is the Supper, a joint meal and exchange, a coembodiment of the body of Christ.

This place exists only as repeated through declaration of the promise and its anamnesis through the Spirit. The promise and its anamnesis is the sacrifice of Jesus. The action of the Supper is a sacrifice, just so. The community is suspended by dwelling in the proclaimed death of Jesus, pleading to God the Father with God the Spirit through the Eucharist. It may seem otherwise, especially given Reformation-era rejection of sacrifice.[38] Yet here ecumenical breakthrough and patristic retrieval at once illuminate how promise and sacrifice are not at odds. Promises require memory, as Nietzsche claimed in his own idiom. Since the pledge, the initial gift, and indeed the bread and wine with their attendant sayings, including the mandates for anamnesis, are public and can be so used to recall the promise offered, to plead with God to fulfill the promise, it is this memory and act of anamnesis

---

36. Jenson, *Systematic Theology*, vol. 2, p. 222.

37. Joint Commission for the Dialogue between the Roman Catholic Church and the Orthodox Church, "The Mystery of the Church and the Eucharist in Light of the Mystery of the Holy Trinity (1982)," in Gros, Meyer, and Rusch, *Growth in Agreement II*, pp. 657-58.

38. On this see Wolfgang Simon, *Die Messopfertheologie Martin Luthers* (Tübingen: Mohr Siebeck, 2003); Karl Lehmann and Wolfhart Pannenberg, eds., *The Condemnations of the Reformation Era: Do They Still Divide?* trans. Margaret Kohl (Minneapolis: Fortress Press, 1990), pp. 84-117.

that is the crux for sacrifice.[39] Rather than considering the Lord's Supper to simply be a place in which one offers the sacrifice of praise, it is indeed a memorial that recalls and therefore represents the self-giving of Jesus. The command to remember is not a command for mere subjective retrieval of the cross and resurrection of Jesus. Rather, as ecumenical dialogue has stated, based upon the pioneering work of the French Groupe des Dombes, this act of memory, undertaken in the Spirit, is an act of return to and representation of the self-giving of Jesus. Since the promise is in this place and the reproducibility of this place occurs through the recollection of this promise, its offering again and again, it is in a sacramental and promissory sense a sacrifice. It is not, as the dialogues have stated, a re-sacrifice of Jesus, as if he had never given himself before. Nor is it a kind of prolongation of the agony of Jesus' self-giving. Rather, on account of the recollection and return to this place, it is a kind of solidarity with or return to the "dangerous memory" of the cross.

Whether and to whom this memory proves dangerous or threatening matters in the public display of promise. If a promise is extended, is delayed, and awaits its fulfillment, those who are promised, its recipients, in the meanwhile must deliberate whether the promise is beneficial or is a threat. Threats and promises have similar formal structures because they both project something into the future. A promise as a gift could also go wrong, its outcome could oppress or be a poisonous and unwelcome thing, just as any gift could. Thus the Eucharist gives us a place of expectation, of awaiting another place.

Finally, the Eucharist gives the place of the neighbor. Since the Eucharist is not its own place, it makes the church out to be no place at all, a place that is porous, anticipatory, and mutual. Likewise, the Eucharist does not give birth to place any differently than the promise, which demands that it be carried on in the impure and ordinary activities of those who trust it. The promise is not handed on in this way and, similarly, the promise's place does not annex others to it. It may leave the other alone and apart when that is needful and when giving or receiving would indeed increase offense and injury instead of ameliorating it. The Eucharist is a moment where promise indeed holds out forgiveness as a future reality but it also demands that Christians take responsibility for their misrecognition of others. Every Christian community needs to recognize its own shortcomings and failures in its own way, its own locale,

---

39. Karl Lehmann and Edmund Schlink, eds., *Das Opfer Jesu Christi und seine Gegenwart in der Kirche* (Göttingen: Vandenhoeck & Ruprecht, 1983), pp. 234-35. See also John D. Zizioulas, *Being as Communion* (Crestwood, NY: St. Vladimir's Seminary Press, 1985), pp. 126-32.

and its own history. The specific failures of the Christian community in the misrecognition of others, its failure to respect religious freedoms, its lack of courage to learn from others or even to simply live indifferently among other religious communities, all this is exposed in the Eucharist. And there Christians can gain strength to face their pasts. Thus, in the complex situation of service, whether it is aid during a crisis or the ordinary grace of offering assistance, Christians can realize that their acts do carry weight and they may be the victims of their own misperception. Thus, the mission and acts of the church can never be divorced from the process of discussion, exchange, and learning from one another. This process is initiated, sustained, and made to be graceful by its suspension in this place.

So, in giving the place of the neighbor, the Eucharist repeats the promise of Jesus in his body and blood because it forms a people who expect, receive, and give even if those chains of giving are broken. The Eucharist occurs as a meal of betrayal. It is celebrated in a middling place, a loaned room, by a cobbled-together list of participants. Just as the Last Supper itself had no properly defined host or boundaries, Christians need not worry about securing themselves a home. Sovereignty often corresponds to rule of a territory and when the Eucharist's topology reflects a kind of ad hoc locale, it resists the ordinary sense of owning a place, of ruling a place, of forcing Christians to be owners of the land while others are without or trespassers. Christians are neither hosts nor guests and resist relationships that would fashion the Eucharist in those terms. Since there is no place located utterly in the past where there are gifts reserved and kept, there is no origin to which to return. One not only leaves the place once occupied, but also seeks out new lands — not in order to extend one's homeland, but to discover new vistas as a guest of others, tutored by them, and awaiting the surprising. One does this while remaining within the promise offered in the Eucharist, aiming at a recognition that is an equal exchange.

In this journey toward the promise that the Eucharist holds out, the church is always on the way to Emmaus. And when he broke bread and they recognized him, he vanished (Luke 24:31).

5.5. Fulfillment

As the Eucharist points to another place, a promised community that is yet to arrive, we conclude with that future. The place of promise is suspended, a kind of place or non-place between the times, much like Johann Georg Hamann described himself at the end of his life as a "man between night and day."[40] Especially in considering the interweaving of promise and time, promise as a doubled and extended gift requires us to consider how that action occurs out of the extension of the promise that Christians dwell between the two poles of the promise, as it were. With attention to place, we have noted that promise anticipates a community to come, that as the Eucharist gathers and disperses, as it disrupts places and drives its participants to the place of the neighbor, we still have that which is to come, that which the Triune God promises. Since Lacoste and Pickstock both invoke the fulfillment, the eschaton, as that which finally drives and liberates us from the ordinary constrictions of place, in the end the Triune God is that End of all things, to which we shall now turn.

Even though promise offers something, the fulfillment of the love of Jesus, it does so by offering a specific person's future; the depiction of the hope engendered by promise does not proceed positively but negatively in what Jesus and his love rejects. This does not exclude the theologian's or the seer's efforts to describe the world that God promises to bring about, the world described variously in the Bible through visions of peace, community, and festival. Robert W. Jenson points out the problem with an an-iconic eschatology that refuses to allow any description of the world to come.[41] Yet this promise does not merely promise as a kind of abstract machinery. If it is a doubled and extended gift, it is a doubled and extended gift of something. A purely formal eschatology that rejects any description would fail as a place of love since it would not admit the neighbor or the community created by the Lord's Supper, anticipatory and atopic though it may be.

To remedy this eschatological aphasia, Jenson draws out the basic form of eschatology: the promise given its content and reality by the crucified and resurrected Jesus is to interpret the hopes and agonies of the communities whom the gospel's missionaries encounter. This, along with two other propositions articulated by Wolfhart Pannenberg, supplies our approach to the place of the Triune God. The first is that eschatological promise must be rendered plausible to humankind; the second is that this promise must finally be God's and rendered by God's power.[42] The first proposition requires eschatological statements to be open to public judgment, a question we treated in the previous section on the Lord's Supper when we considered that the Supper's claims

40. Johann Georg Hamann, "Letztes Blatt" (1788), in *Kreuz und Kritik: Johann Georg Hamanns Letztes Blatt,* ed. Oswald Bayer and Christian Knudsen (Tübingen: Mohr Siebeck, 1983), p. 56.

41. Jenson, *Systematic Theology,* vol. 2, pp. 311-12.

42. Wolfhart Pannenberg, "Constructive and Critical Functions of Christian Eschatology," *Harvard Theological Review* 77 (1984): 119-39.

and actions are open to judgment to discern whether that which the Supper promises is indeed a beneficial promise and not a threat. The second proposition is a largely negative one that requires a claim that the promised world is indeed achieved by God and not by the immanent possibilities of the world. Thus, these two propositions offer a way to consider eschatological claims that indeed do address human situations but are not merely wish fulfillment.

Considering promise as a doubled and extended gift allows us to see how it both addresses the given hopes into which the gospel steps in the sense that Jenson describes, interpreting these hopes by the promise of Jesus, and also how it operates in the negative and weak sense we describe without bringing the aleatoric and eschatologically unexpected to heel.[43] Because the promise is primarily critical of negative situations of power and economy, because it introduces this impulse, it is proper to consider how promise offers a primarily negative or critical hope. The future of promise, its fulfillment, likewise should be driven by the same moral *sensorium* that serves the neighbor in the meanwhile. To stress the critical hope of promise does not mean that the promise will bring with it permanence and eternal negative relation to what is rejected. Such a situation would mean that the promise is finally negative and does not deliver what it offers, that is, theosis, or participation in the life of the Triune God. Rather, understanding the promised place of the future through its reversal will show how promise is remembrance as well as what "no eye has seen, nor ear heard" (1 Cor. 2:9).

Because the Supper occurs, yet again, in the night of betrayal, it occurs with a view toward damaged community and failed hope. Because it does not offer certainty in the sense that a strong promise would, it does not claim that these failings will find their redemption. But since the atopic character of the Supper opens out to the place of the neighbor, the place for developing a critical hope is through attention to the injuries possessed by the neighbor. To this we may claim that the promised life of God would reject that which injured and set aside that which damages. But since the place of the Triune God is no other place than this atopic Supper, eschatological claims are claims that are other-directed and attentive to the plurality of what the neighbor needs. The interpretive and rhetorical task given by this eschatology is to consider how the promise of God delivered in bread and wine is a promise that either makes room for the neighbor, to include the stranger or outsider within the Eucharistic community, to discover in the neighbor as of yet unheard of gifts or surprising judgments — or, on the other hand, to leave the neighbor as-is,

---

43. Jenson states several criteria to separate wish-fulfillment from eschatological statements in *Systematic Theology*, vol. 2, pp. 317-19.

to make the promise beneficial to the neighbor in her or his understanding, to repent of failed efforts to serve the other, and to leave the other alone when needed. This is to expect the future with the weak power that is God's promise.

This qualification of where promise occurs makes it readily available, as close as bread and wine. The promise takes place in this Supper, and so if promise is the way in which God deals with us, the Lord's Supper is where God takes place. Even though the Eucharist is atopic and gives the place of the neighbor, it is ultimately the place of God as the *arrabon* of the promise of God. Whether it is, and whether we might judge it true, depends entirely on God's keeping of the promise. Unless it proves empty, we may continue to remember it, dwell in it, and act from it, living as "one between night and day."

Bibliography

Agamben, Giorgio. *Homo Sacer: Sovereign Power and Bare Life.* Translated by Daniel Heller-Roazen. Ştanford: Stanford University Press, 1998.

———. "On Potentiality." In *Potentialities: Collected Essays in Philosophy.* Edited and translated by Daniel Heller-Roazen, 177-84. Stanford: Stanford University Press, 1999.

Allnutt, Gillian. "Sarah's Laughter." In *How the Bicycle Shone: New and Selected Poems.* Tarset: Bloodaxe Books, 2007.

Arendt, Hannah. *The Human Condition.* Chicago: University of Chicago Press, 1989.

Arterbury, Andrew E. "Abraham's Hospitality among Jewish and Early Christian Writers." *Perspectives in Religious Studies* 30 (2006): 359-76.

Assel, Heinrich. "Verheissung." In *Historisches Wörterbuch der Philosophie.* Volume 11, 689-94. Basel: Schwabe Verlag, 2001.

Austin, J. L. *How to Do Things with Words.* 2nd edition. Edited by J. O. Urmson and Marina Sbisà. Cambridge: Harvard University Press, 1975.

Barth, Karl. *Der Römerbrief, Zweite Fassung 1922.* Zürich: Theologischer Verlag, 1989.

Bayer, Oswald. "Categorical Imperative or Categorical Gift?" In *Freedom in Response: Lutheran Ethics; Sources and Controversies.* Translated by Jeffrey F. Cayzer, 13-20. Oxford: Oxford University Press, 2007.

———. "Ethik der Gabe." In *Die Gabe: Ein "Urwort" der Theologie?* Edited by Veronika Hoffmann, 99-124. Frankfurt: Verlag Otto Lembeck, 2009.

———. *Martin Luther's Theology: A Contemporary Interpretation.* Translated by Thomas H. Trapp. Grand Rapids: Eerdmans, 2008.

———. *Promissio: Geschichte der reformatischen Wende in Luthers Theologie.* 2nd ed. Darmstadt: Wissenschaftliche Buchgesellschaft, 1989.

———. "Rechtfertigungslehre und Ontologie." In *Zugesagte Gegenwart,* 196-205. Tübingen: Mohr Siebeck, 2007.

———. *Theologie.* Gütersloh: Gütersloher Verlagshaus, 1994.

Benjamin, Walter. "On the Concept of History." In *Selected Writings,* volume 4: *1938-1940.* Edited by Howard Eiland and Michael W. Jennings. Translated by Edmund Jephcott et al., 389-400. Cambridge, MA: Belknap, 2003.

Benveniste, Emile. *Indo-European Language and Society.* Translated by Elizabeth Palmer. Coral Gables: University of Miami Press, 1973.

Bernstein, Richard J. *Beyond Objectivism and Relativism: Science, Hermeneutics, and Praxis.* Philadelphia: University of Pennsylvania Press, 1988.

Bertram, Robert W. *A Time for Confessing.* Edited by Michael Hoy. Grand Rapids: Eerdmans, 2008.

The Book of Concord: The Confessions of the Evangelical Lutheran Church. Edited by Robert Kolb and Timothy J. Wengert. Translated by Charles Arand et al. Minneapolis: Fortress Press, 2000.

Bourdieu, Pierre. *Outline of a Theory of Practice.* Translated by Richard Nice. Cambridge: Cambridge University Press, 1977.

Bradshaw, Paul N. *The Search for the Origins of Christian Worship.* 2nd edition. Oxford: Oxford University Press, 2002.

Camenisch, Paul F. "Gift and Gratitude in Ethics." *Journal of Religious Ethics* 9 (1981): 1-34.

Caputo, John D. *Deconstruction in a Nutshell: A Conversation with Jacques Derrida.* New York: Fordham University Press, 1997.

———. *Demythologizing Heidegger.* Bloomington: Indiana University Press, 1993.

———. *The Prayers and Tears of Jacques Derrida: Religion without Religion.* Bloomington: Indiana University Press, 1997.

———. *The Weakness of God: A Theology of the Event.* Bloomington: Indiana University Press, 2006.

Carey, Edward S. *The Fate of Place: A Philosophical History.* Berkeley: University of California Press, 1997.

Chilton, Bruce. *A Feast of Meanings: Eucharistic Theologies from Jesus through Johannine Circles.* Leiden: Brill, 1994.

Coakley, Sarah. "Why Gift? Gift, Gender, and Trinitarian Relations in Tanner and Milbank." *Scottish Journal of Theology* 61 (2008): 224-35.

Courtine, Jean-François. *Inventio analogiae: Métaphysique et ontothéologie.* Paris: Vrin, 2005.

Cunningham, Conor. *Genealogy of Nihilism.* London: Routledge, 2000.

Derrida, Jacques. "Avances." In Serge Margel, *Le tombeau du dieu artisan,* 11-43. Paris: Minuit, 1995.

———. *Given Time: 1. Counterfeit Money.* Translated by Peggy Kamuf. Chicago: University of Chicago Press, 1992.

————. "Réponses de Jacques Derrida." In *La Philosophie au risqué de la promesse*. Edited by Marc Crépon and Marc de Launay, 197-98. Paris: Bayard, 2004.

————. "Signature Event Context." In *Limited, Inc.* Translated by Samuel Weber and Jeffrey Mehlman, 1-24. Evanston: Northwestern University Press, 1988.

————. "Une Hospitalité à L'Infini." In *Manifeste pour l'Hospitalité*. Edited by Michel Wieviorka and Mohammed Seffahi, 97-106. Grigny: Paroles D'Aube, 1999.

Derrida, Jacques, and Anne Dufourmantelle. *On Hospitality: Anne Dufourmantelle Invites Jacques Derrida to Respond*. Translated by Rachel Bowlby. Stanford: Stanford University Press, 2000.

Foucault, Michel. "Qu'est-ce que la critique? Critique et Aufklärung." *Bulletin de la Société française de Philosophie* 84 (1990): 35-63.

Gell, Alfred. *The Anthropology of Time: Cultural Constructions of Temporal Maps and Images*. Providence: Berg, 1992.

Godelier, Maurice. *The Enigma of Gift*. Translated by Nora Scott. Chicago: University of Chicago Press, 1999.

Goudbout, Jacques T., and Alain Caillé. *The World of the Gift*. Translated by Donald Winkler. Montreal and Kingston: McGill-Queen's University Press, 1998.

Grosz, Elizabeth. *Space, Time, and Perversion*. London: Routledge, 1995.

Groupe des Dombes. "L'Esprit Saint, L'Eglise et les Sacraments (1979)." In *Pour la communion des Eglises: L'apport du Groupe des Dombes (1937-1987)*. Edited by Alain Blancy and Maurice Jourjon, 115-56. Paris: Editions du Centurion, 1988.

Habermas, Jürgen. *Der philosophisches Diskurs der Moderne: Zwölf Vorlesungen*. Frankfurt: Suhrkamp Verlag, 1991.

Hahn, Ferdinand. "Zum Stand der Erforschung des urchristlichen Herrenmahls." *Evangelische Theologie* 35 (1975): 553-63.

Hamann, Johann Georg. "Letztes Blatt (1788)." In *Kreuz und Kritik: Johann Georg Hamanns Letztes Blatt*. Edited by Oswald Bayer and Christian Knudsen, 52-63. Tübingen: Mohr Siebeck, 1983.

Hamm, Berndt. *Promissio, Pactum, Ordinatio: Freiheit und Selbstbindung Gottes in der scholastischen Gnadenlehre*. Tübingen: Mohr Siebeck, 1977.

Heidegger, Martin. "Building, Dwelling, Thinking." In *Poetry, Language, and Thought*. Translated by Albert Hofstadter, 143-62. New York: Harper & Row, 1971.

————. "Kunst und Raum." In *Aus der Erfahrung des Denkens*, vol. 13 of *Gesamtausgabe*. Edited by Hermann Heidegger, 203-10. Frankfurt: Klostermann, 1983.

————. "Seminar in Le Thor, 1969." In *Seminare*, vol. 15 of *Gesamtausgabe*. Edited by Curd Ochwadt, 326-71. Frankfurt: Klostermann Verlag, 1986.

————. "The Thing." In *Poetry, Language, and Thought*. Translated by Albert Hofstadter, 163-86. New York: Harper & Row, 1971.

————. "Zeit und Sein." In *Zur Sache des Denkens*, 1-26. Tübingen: Max Niemeyer, 1969.

Hénaff, Marcel. *The Price of Truth: Gift, Money, and Philosophy*. Translated by Jean-Louis Morhange. Stanford: Stanford University Press, 2010.

Henrikson, Jan-Olav. *Desire, Gift, and Recognition: Christology and Postmodern Philosophy*. Grand Rapids: Eerdmans, 2009.

Hobbs, T. R. "Hospitality in the First Testament and the 'Teleological Fallacy.'" *Journal for the Study of the Old Testament* 95 (2001): 3-30.

Hoffmann, Veronika, ed. *Die Gabe: Ein "Urwort" der Theologie?* Frankfurt: Verlag Otto Lembeck, 2009.

Holm, Bo Kristian, and Peter Widmann, eds. *Word-Gift-Being: Justification-Economy-Ontology*. Tübingen: Mohr Siebeck, 2009.

Honneth, Axel. "Recognition as Ideology." In *Recognition and Power: Axel Honneth and the Tradition of Critical Social Theory*. Edited by Bert van den Brink and David Owen, 323-47. Cambridge: Cambridge University Press, 2007.

————. *The Struggle for Recognition: The Moral Grammar of Social Conflicts*. Translated by Joel Anderson. Cambridge: MIT Press, 1995.

Hoy, David Couzens. *The Time of Our Lives: A Critical History of Temporality*. Cambridge: MIT Press, 2009.

Hume, David. *A Treatise of Human Nature*. Edited by P. H. Nidditch. Oxford: Oxford University Press, 1978.

Hütter, Reinhard. *Suffering Divine Things: Theology as Church Practice*. Translated by Doug Stott. Grand Rapids: Eerdmans, 1997.

Hyde, Lewis. *The Gift: Imagination and the Erotic Life of Property*. New York: Vintage, 1983.

International Lutheran–Roman Catholic Dialogue. *Joint Declaration on the Doctrine of Justification*. In *Growth in Agreement II: Reports and Agreed Statements of Ecumenical Conversations on a World Level, 1982-1998*. Edited by Jeffrey Gros, Harding Meyer, and William G. Rusch, 566-82. Grand Rapids: Eerdmans.

Irigaray, Luce. *An Ethics of Sexual Difference*. Translated by Carolyn Burke and Gillian C. Gill. Ithaca: Cornell University Press, 1993.

Jenson, Robert W. *Story and Promise: A Brief Theology of the Gospel*. Philadelphia: Fortress Press, 1973.

————. *Systematic Theology*. 2 volumes. Oxford: Oxford University Press, 1997, 2000.

Jervall, Jacob. "Sons of the Prophets: The Holy Spirit in the Acts of the Apostles." In *The Unknown Paul: Essays on Luke-Acts and Early Christian History*, 96-121. Minneapolis: Augsburg Press, 1984.

Joint Commission for the Dialogue between the Roman Catholic Church and the Orthodox Church. "The Mystery of the Church and the Eucharist in Light of the Mystery of the Holy Trinity." In *Growth in Agreement II: Reports and Agreed Statements of Ecumenical Conversations on a World Level, 1982-1998*. Edited by Jeffrey Gros, Harding Meyer, and William G. Rusch, 652-59. Grand Rapids: Eerdmans, 2000.

Jüngel, Eberhard. *Gott als Geheimnis der Welt: Zur Begründung der Theologie des Gekreuzigten im Streit zwischen Theismus und Atheismus*. Tübingen: Mohr Siebeck, 1977.

―――. "Die Welt als Möglichkeit und Wirklichkeit. Zum ontologischen Ansatz der Rechtfertigungslehre." In *Unterwegs zur Sache*, 3rd ed., 206-33. Tübingen: Mohr Siebeck, 2000.

Kant, Immanuel. "What Does It Mean to Orient Oneself in Thinking?" In *Religion and Rational Theology*. Edited and translated by Allen W. Wood and George Di Giovanni, 1-18. Cambridge: Cambridge University Press, 1996.

Kearney, Richard. *The God Who May Be: The Hermeneutics of Religion*. Bloomington: Indiana University Press, 2001.

Keifert, Patrick R. *Welcoming the Stranger: A Public Theology of Worship and Evangelism*. Minneapolis: Fortress Press, 1992.

Knuth, Hans Christian, ed. *Angeklagt und Anerkannt: Luthers Rechtfertigungslehre in gegenwärtiger Verantwortung*. Erlangen: Martin-Luther-Verlag, 2009.

Lacoste, Jean-Yves. *Expérience et absolu: Questions disputées sur l'humanité de l'homme*. Paris: Presses Universitaires de France, 1994.

Lehmann, Karl, and Edmund Schlink, eds. *Das Opfer Jesu Christi und seine Gegenwart in der Kirche*. Göttingen: Vandenhoeck & Ruprecht, 1983.

Lehmann, Karl, and Wolfhart Pannenberg, eds. *The Condemnations of the Reformation Era: Do They Still Divide?* Translated by Margaret Kohl. Minneapolis: Fortress Press, 1990.

Levinas, Emmanuel. "Heidegger, Gagarin, and Us." In *Difficult Freedom: Essays on Judaism*. Translated by Séan Hand, 231-34. Baltimore: Johns Hopkins University Press, 1990.

―――. "Le trace d'Autre." *Tijdschrift voor filosofie* 25 (1963): 605-23.

Lévi-Strauss, Claude. "Introduction à l'oeuvre de Marcel Mauss." In Marcel Mauss, *Sociologie et Anthropologie*. Edited by Georges Gurvitch, ix-lii. Paris: Presses Universitaires de France, 1950.

Lincoln, Andrew. *Truth on Trial: The Lawsuit Motif in John's Gospel*. Grand Rapids: Baker Academic, 2000.

Luther, Martin. "Bondage of the Will." In *Luther and Erasmus: Free Will and Sal-*

vation. Edited by E. Gordon Rupp and Philip S. Watson. Translated by E. Gordon Rupp et al., 101-333. Philadelphia: Westminster Press, 1969.

———. *Freedom of a Christian.* Translated by Mark Tranvik. Minneapolis: Fortress Press, 2006.

Malina, Bruce J. "The Received View and What It Cannot Do: III John and Hospitality." *Semeia* 35 (1986): 171-86.

Malinowski, Bronislaw. *Argonauts of the Western Pacific.* New York: Dutton, 1953.

Malpas, Jeffrey. "Geography, Biology, and Politics." In *Heidegger and the Thinking of Place: Explorations in the Topology of Being,* 137-58. Cambridge: MIT Press, 2011.

———. *Heidegger's Topology: Being, Place, World.* Cambridge: MIT Press, 2006.

———. *Place and Experience: A Philosophical Topography.* Cambridge: Cambridge University Press, 1999.

Manoussakis, John Panteleimon. *God After Metaphysics: A Theological Aesthetic.* Bloomington: Indiana University Press, 2007.

Marion, Jean-Luc. *Being Given: Toward a Phenomenology of Givenness.* Translated by Jeffrey L. Kosky. Stanford: Stanford University Press, 2002.

Matthews, Victor H., and Don C. Benjamin. "The Host and the Stranger." In *The Social World of Ancient Israel, 1250-587 BCE,* 83-85. Peabody: Hendrickson Publishers, 1993.

Mauss, Marcel. *The Gift: The Form and Reason for Exchange in Archaic Society.* Translated by W. D. Halls. New York: Norton, 1990.

Milbank, John. *Being Reconciled: Ontology and Pardon.* London: Routledge, 2003.

———. "Can a Gift Be Given? Prolegomena to a Future Trinitarian Metaphysic." *Modern Theology* 11 (1995): 119-59.

———. "The Thing Given." *Archivio di filosofia* 74 (2006): 503-39.

———. "The Transcendentality of the Gift: A Summary." In *The Future of Love: Essays in Political Theology,* 352-63. Eugene: Cascade Books, 2009.

Moltmann, Jürgen. *Theologie der Hoffnung: Untersuchungen zur Begründung und zu den Konsequenzen einer christlichen Eschatologie.* Munich: Chr. Kaiser Verlag, 1965.

Morse, Christopher. *The Logic of Promise in Moltmann's Theology.* Philadelphia: Fortress Press, 1979.

Niederwimmer, Kurt. *The Didache: A Commentary.* Edited by Harold W. Attridge. Translated by Linda M. Maloney. Minneapolis: Fortress Press, 1998.

Nietzsche, Friedrich. *On the Genealogy of Morality.* Edited by Keith Ansell-Pearson. Translated by Carol Diethe. Cambridge: Cambridge University Press, 2007.

Ouspensky, Leonid, and Vladimir Lossky. *The Meaning of Icons.* Translated by G. E. H. Palmer and E. Kadloubovsky. Crestwood, NY: St. Vladimir's Seminary Press, 1982.

Pannenberg, Wolfhart. "Constructive and Critical Functions of Christian Eschatology." *Harvard Theological Review* 77 (1984): 119-39.

―――. "Dogmatische Thesen zur Lehre von der Offenbarung." In *Offenbarung als Geschichte*. Edited by Wolfhart Pannenberg, 91-114. Göttingen: Vandenhoeck & Ruprecht, 1965.

―――. "Die Rechtfertigungslehre im okumenischen Gesprach." In *Beiträge zur systematischen Theologie*. Volume 3, 275-88. Göttingen: Vandenhoeck & Ruprecht, 1999.

Pickstock, Catherine. *After Writing: On the Liturgical Consummation of Philosophy*. Oxford: Blackwell, 1998.

Pitt-Rivers, Julian. "The Law of Hospitality." In *The Fate of Schechem, or the Politics of Sex: Essays in the Anthropology of the Mediterranean*, 107-12. Cambridge: Cambridge University Press, 1977.

Pohl, Christine D. *Making Room: Recovering Hospitality as a Christian Tradition*. Grand Rapids: Eerdmans, 1999.

Power, David N. *Sacrament: The Language of God's Giving*. New York: Herder & Herder, 1999.

Rad, Gerhard von. *Das Opfer des Abrahams*. Munich: Chr. Kaiser Verlag, 1971.

Reinhuber, Thomas. *Kämpfender Glaube: Studien zu Luthers Bekenntnis am Ende von* De servo arbitrio. Berlin: Walter de Gruyter, 2000.

Ricoeur, Paul. *Amour et justice*. Paris: Seuil, 2008.

―――. *Parcours de la reconnaissance: Trois études*. Paris: Gallimard, 2001.

Rorty, Richard. *Philosophy and the Mirror of Nature*. Oxford: Blackwell Publishers, 1980.

Sahlins, Marshal. *Stone Age Economics*. London: Routledge, 2004.

Scharlemann, Robert. "Constructing Theological Models." *Journal of Religion* 53 (1973): 63-82.

Schrag, Calvin O. *God as Otherwise Than Being: Toward a Semantics of the Gift*. Evanston: Northwestern University Press, 2002.

Simon, Wolfgang. *Die Messopfertheologie Martin Luthers*. Tübingen: Mohr Siebeck, 2003.

Simpson, Gary M. *Critical Social Theory: Prophetic Reason, Civil Society, and Christian Imagination*. Minneapolis: Fortress Press, 2002.

Smith, Dennis E. *From Symposium to Eucharist: The Banquet in the Early Christian World*. Minneapolis: Fortress Press, 2003.

Sykes, Karen Margaret. *Arguing with Anthropology: An Introduction to Critical Theories of the Gift*. London: Routledge, 2005.

Tanner, Kathryn. *Economy of Grace*. Minneapolis: Fortress Press, 2005.

―――. *Jesus, Humanity, and the Trinity: A Brief Systematic Theology*. Minneapolis: Fortress Press, 2001.

————. *Theories of Culture: A New Agenda for Theology.* Minneapolis: Fortress Press, 1997.

Taylor, Charles. *A Secular Age.* Cambridge: Belknap, 2007.

Thiel, John E. *Nonfoundationalism.* Minneapolis: Fortress Press, 2000.

Thunberg, Lars. "Early Christian Interpretations of the Three Angels in Gen. 18." *Studia Patristica* 7 (1966): 560-70.

Toulmin, Stephen. *Cosmopolis: The Hidden Agenda of Modernity.* Chicago: University of Chicago Press, 1990.

van Huyssteen, J. Wentzel. *The Shaping of Rationality: Toward Interdisciplinarity in Theology and Science.* Grand Rapids: Eerdmans, 1999.

Wall, John. *Moral Creativity: Paul Ricoeur and the Poetics of Possibility.* Oxford: Oxford University Press, 2005.

Walter, Gregory. "Critique and Promise in Paul Tillich's Political Theology: Engaging Giorgio Agamben on Sovereignty and Possibility." *Journal of Religion* 90 (2010): 453-74.

————. "An Introduction to Hans Joachim Iwand's *The Righteousness of Faith According to Luther.*" *Lutheran Quarterly* 21 (2007): 17-26.

————. "Karl Holl (1866-1926) and the Recovery of Promise in Luther." *Lutheran Quarterly* 25 (2011): 398-413.

Ward, Graham. *Cultural Transformation and Religious Practice.* Cambridge: Cambridge University Press, 2005.

Webb, Stephen H. *The Gifting God: A Trinitarian Ethics of Excess.* Oxford: Oxford University Press, 1996.

Weiner, Annette B. *Inalienable Possessions: The Paradox of Keeping-While-Giving.* Berkeley: University of California Press, 1992.

Westermann, Claus. *Genesis: 12–36.* Translated by John J. Sullion, S.J. Minneapolis: Fortress Press, 1995.

Westhelle, Vitor. *The Church Event: Call and Challenge of a Church Protestant.* Minneapolis: Fortress Press, 2010.

Williams, Rowan. *Resurrection: Interpreting the Easter Gospel.* Revised edition. Cleveland: Pilgrim Press, 2002.

Zizioulas, John D. *Being as Communion.* Crestwood, NY: St. Vladimir's Seminary Press, 1985.

Index